The 9 to 5 Side Hustler:

A Guide to Balancing Your Day Job With Your Small Business

By Kris McPeak

The 9 to 5 Side Hustle: A Guide to Balancing Your Day Job With Your Small Business

This book is dedicated to my sister, Jennifer Mayer Jordan. She has always been my side hustle inspiration and I could not have written this book without her love and support.

(Now I'm going back to the game...that's a private joke)

Special Thanks...

There are a whole hell of a lot of peeps who got me to this place, where I feel more than ever like I've got something to say and that the world needs to hear it. So there.

To the #27Bestsellers - yo, we are doing it!!

To Dr. Erika Endrijonas - thank you for "Semper Gumby."

To my Appreciation Rant Buddies and RBMM Gals - Janice and Tamar - there is no way in hell I'm here right now without having you ladies in my ear every day, telling me to just fucking get it done. I love you guys.

To my supervisor, mentor, and Personal Obi Wan, Bobbi Abram, who helps me draw the line while making sure I stop defending my limitations. To quote Michelle Branch, "You Get Me." Thanks again for saving me from The Dark Side.

To my teammates with SilverPeak Performance...

y'all keep me #sppstrong

To my hubby, Charles - thanks for always being the Coolest Guy in the Universe and reminding me that I really can do hard things. I love you so much.

READER BONUS

Check out my website to access the reader bonus content!

You Need a Time Budget - FREE
Top 22 Ways to Get More Done and Elevate Your 8 - FREE

Home by 5:
How to Thrive in Your Dream Job and Achieve Time Freedom
20% off when you use the coupon code
9TO5

Find it all at www.krismcpeak.com/ 9to5book

Praise for the Author

Kris has inspired and motivated me to get more done in less hours and she shares some great tips on how to do so. Kris is authentic and full of energy!"
Paula Miller, Lost AF Wellness Podcast

As a person who's self-employed and working from home, time management and work-life balance can be a real struggle for me. I'm so happy that I found a podcast to help me get my act together. Kris and her guests make me feel motivated and have given me many great tips.
Alana Haldan - Sprouts and Krauts

Be Safe. Stay Home and Read This.
Once again, my friend and author Kris McPeak has created something you need to experience for yourself. Reading her work is like having a conversation with a friend and mentor. You will laugh a lot, you may cry a little, but you will certainly learn from the experience. She has detailed simple, practical steps for someone who wants to hustle 24 hours a day, but may need to

rethink their approach. From time management techniques to sleep research, she will help the reader remain somewhat calm in these challenging times. Buy the book today, take action tomorrow....you won't regret it.

P.S. Keep a pen and paper handy for all the authors, apps and websites she mentions.

Doug Ferguson, Director of Development, Delaware Valley Community College

This show had me leaning in an wanting to hear more! Kris speaks with authority and heart. Her episodes are super helpful and I feel like I'm listening to a friend share great advice. She's really good at interviewing and brings on interesting guests.

Whitney Lauritsen (The Eco Vegan Gal) - Host of "This Might Get Uncomfortable"

Kris has inspired me to do more and be more as I now know how to be more efficient with my time! A Must Listen!

Janice McQueen - Host of "Beauty Call Podcast"

This book includes vulnerable tales of triumph

and defeat in the workplace and a conscious quest to reframe paradigms in order to build sustainable time management strategies. All of this, in the name of pursuing passion projects (side hustles) without quitting your day job. Kris is the real deal. No B.S. and all heart.

-J.B.Harrington - Career Advisor at California State University - Chico

Kris has a fun personality that she effortlessly brings to this podcast to provide quick and enjoyable ways to get more out of the 24 hours a day we all have.

Marisa Imon - Host of "Incandescent"

We need more women like Kris! She has a gift of showing multi-passionate women how to not feel guilty about going after their dreams. Kris shows us that it is absolutely possible to have a full time career AND a successful small business. You don't have to choose - you can have both! Thank you, Kris, for showing us how to balance it all!

Lindsay Maloney - Host of "Book Your Dream Clients" podcast

* * *

I LOVE the concept of Elevating your 8! There is a quote I heard recently that said something to the effect of, "We all have the same amount of hours in a day as Beyonce." I laughed, but this is true of every human being. We may all have different origin stories, background and life experiences, but we all have the same amount of TIME. So when it put it into perspective that way, I realized that there must be a better way to make the best, most productive use of our time so we can create extraordinary things the world! This is where Kris McPeak comes in! Kris teaches us the tricks, tools, and tips to elevate our 8 hours every day with inspiring interviews, great guests, and a unique perspective. I am so happy to add this podcast to my permanent rotation.

Allison Melody - Host of "Food Heals Podcast"

Introduction

FIRST OF ALL:

Let me tell you about the incredibly taxing conversation I had in my head about my title, The 9 to 5 Side HUSTLER.

"Kris, that's just a little bit polarizing."
"People are going to think about Larry Flynt and strippers."
"No one says 'Side Hustlers,' they say, 'Side Hustle.'"

And so on, and so on, and so on.

And then I happened upon Ramit Sethi's website… which was not on accident. While he's a stark-raving millennial, I'm a crotchety Gen Xer, but I love his work, his writing, his sense of humor. Ramit is a genius.

* * *

I read his book, I Will Teach You to Be Rich, when my sister (same sister in the dedication) shared her Audible account with me. I had heard Gen X friends of mine tell me that I would not enjoy this book; that Ramit was kind of a snot. But as you'll learn shortly, I have had money mindset issues for years. I listened to Ramit's book and learned something cool about him that applied directly to some of what I do in my day job.

In that day job, I run a scholarship program at a community college (among other things), and Ramit's story about preparing for college and applying for scholarships is quite impressive.

Ramit's parents told him that if he was going to go to college, he'd need to apply for a lot of scholarships. So he did. He went to his high school counseling office every day and looked up scholarship applications. He spent one to two hours every day working on scholarship applications. He found his niche in how to write scholarship essays (write about what his peers would NOT write about). By the time Ramit was ready for his freshman year, he had earned about $100,000 in scholarships. He attended Stanford University with no debt. And then, you might say, the rest is history.

Anyway, I was looking up this story because I wanted to include it in my Fall 2020 Scholarship Workshop slideshow, and I happened upon one of Ramit's quizzes. His opt-in. The lead magnet that's used to get people onto his mailing list so they will eventually buy things (which I have been known to do with Ramit and several other online entrepreneurs).

The quiz I took is called, "What's Your Earning Potential?" And I discovered that I fall into a category called "The Hustler."

Ramit is quick to explain that I'm not going to be working the blackjack table anytime soon (or playing pool with Fast Eddie Felson, although that would be cool—RIP Paul Newman). And then he said THIS:

Characteristics of The Hustler.

As a lifelong learner and doer, you don't need a quiz to tell you that you are constantly trying to improve. Whether in your personal or professional life, you are always trying to be the best and experience the best life has to offer. You are never complacent—you are firmly on the path of self-development.

You feel that life is a journey of learning.

You constantly feel like there's more in life for you and you are always looking for opportunities to grow and learn something new. Even if you can settle for some periods, there will always be something else to chase - the next big thing for you.

As a Hustler, you...

1. Know there's more to life and are always striving for the next challenge.

2. Are fiercely independent, but you know you can't do it all yourself. You work best on a team of A-players.

3. Are a strong, caring person...but if someone breaks your trust, you are quick to move on.

4. Are creative, although not necessarily an artist - your creativity often shows up in more subtle and practical ways.

You find yourself often overflowed with ideas. There's no shortage of options and ideas for you and often the hard part is to pick the right one at the right moment. Frustration is not unknown to you as you often struggle to find the right resources to execute on all those great ideas.

You always end up getting there.

* * *

You always find a way to go around whatever is in the way of your goals. You're confident that even if you don't have a direct answer to a problem, you know you'll find a way to solve it.

As a Hustler, you're constantly looking for the smartest way to solve a problem with the minimum amount of time and energy invested. It's common for you to have tons of tabs open in your browser. Watch out, though, as often you find yourself stuck trying to find the "right" option.

Well, shit. If that didn't hit me over the top of the head with a cast-iron frying pan and leave me for dead. I have since read that section of text about a thousand times. Here's what always grabs me:

- Lifelong learner and doer—**Yup.**

- Creative although not artistic—**You know it.**

- Looking for the smartest way to solve a

problem with the minimum amount of time and energy invested—**Oh, hell yeah.**

◆ Strong, caring person with multiple tabs open on the browser—**How the fuck did he know?**

So, yeah, the title of this book and the person I'm writing about is a total Side HUSTLER.

Not a Larry Flynt, J-Lo, or New Jack Hustler. A 9-to-5 Side Hustler.

Let's move on…

Having a side hustle for me was originally about making money. From lemonade stands in grade school to "experimenting" with Mary Kay and The Body Shop… from selling on Amazon and eBay to using sites like Gazelle and DeCluttr. And there was even the dreaded second job(s). I wanted to make more money because I felt like I never had any.

I've always had a job of some sort since I was in the ninth grade. That summer I became a housekeeper for a local motel owned by a friend of the family. I loved this family; they were like my second set of parents a lot of the time. It was a motel in a small town in rural Arkansas. So I don't have to tell you that I cleaned up after a great deal of one-night stands. But I did learn a solid work ethic from this gig, and I'm pretty proud of having started work early in my life.

From housekeeper to waitress when the motel expanded and built a restaurant… and I learned the value of tips (which I would blow off later when I was in grad school, but that's another story). And then, the summer between my first and second year of college, I worked at Tyson Foods in "further processing." Oh, joy. My father was an employee there and it was the best gig a student could get because of the hourly wage. Pop had set up an interview for me and my boyfriend at the time, and we were hired together on the second shift, in Further Processing. Further Processing is anything frozen that needs to be packaged, but I worked a few nights here and there in other sections, some of which were easier than others. We worked daily from four-thirty p.m. to one-thirty a.m. Two fifteen-minute breaks and thirty minutes for "lunch." I'm not going to say those were the worst days of my life… but I will say that it took a couple of years for me to enjoy eating poultry products again. And I didn't even work close to any of the truly nasty stuff! Although, my boyfriend always insisted that I drink root beer before driving back home so I could stay awake; and while he was pretty much one of the smartest people I ever knew in my life, he never understood that root beer doesn't have any caffeine.

But I digress.

After my summer at Tyson Foods, I spend the next four summers working in Chicago with my stepmother at the Freeman Decorating Company. They are a tradeshow company. And you probably don't know what I mean by that unless you've done it before. But surely you're familiar with car shows and bridal shows, stuff like that. FDC provides all the trimmings and labor for those events. Need a booth set up? Freeman will do it. Need to rent trashcans and furniture for your booth? Freeman. Check-in stations? Yup. This was some of the hardest work I ever did, and we worked some pretty long hours. But I made some incredible friends, made more money than I did at Tyson Foods, AND spent these summers in my very favorite city—Chicago. Having grown up in the suburbs of Chicago, it was magic to spend time with my old friends, make new ones, and score additional funding for the next school year.

* * *

When I became an RA (that's resident assistant/ resident advisor for those of you unfamiliar with campus housing), I entered a field that would become my career, although I didn't realize it at the time. And while it was a job, it never really felt like one. During these years, I didn't get paid hourly or anything like that—just a stipend at the end of the semester. Our room and board were covered. If you wanted to make hourly wages you could "volunteer" for security shifts during the week. Security in those days meant sitting out on a cot from ten p.m. to seven a.m., checking key codes when students came back to the building, and locking the doors at midnight. Which then also meant having to get up from the cot to open the door, check the keys, and possibly go back to sleep. That's right. Security, with cots, and you could sleep (it was the '80's—don't judge). Now and then a fire alarm would go off or an intoxicated person would come home and we wouldn't let them in the residence hall; we'd call Public Safety instead.

Being an RA felt much more like socializing and hanging out, because I got to plan programs for my residents, go to on-campus events, sometimes travel to a conference, and occasionally have to do a write-up if someone was misbehaving. I LOVED being part of the staff. Fall and Spring Training were like a party. We did skits, went camping, and then eventually made our way to "behind closed doors," which was roleplaying potential situations so you could practice how you might solve the problem. Ah… those were the days.

For Senior Year #1 (yes, I had a Super Senior Year), I moved off campus to have that experience as well as participate in a very high-level extracurricular activity that would have clashed with the RA position. I took a few different part-time jobs to help pay the bills here and there, although I didn't love them. At Sears, I sold computers, vacuums, sewing machines, typewriters, and telephones. I earned commissions plus my hourly rate. I was NOT good at sales, but most people come to Sears knowing what they want, so I did okay. I also tried my hand at a fast-food gig working as a non-roller-skating carhop at a Sonic Drive-In. That job lasted exactly five hours. I worked one shift and never went back.

After graduation, I went straight to graduate school. My degree was in secondary education, but along the way during my RA years, someone told me that you could make a living doing this. WHAT? I can plan parties and events and go to training and conferences and sometimes write someone up and you'll PAY me for that? I'm totally in! But first, graduate school. Oh… all right. You're going to pay for my graduate school? Plus my housing AND a monthly stipend? Where do I sign up?

* * *

Most of my hall director colleagues were majoring in student affairs administration, but that particular program was not calling to me, so I chose the longer route—counselor education. And when those three years of grad school were over, I'd made up my mind to become a student affairs professional.

Why do I tell you all of this? Because the pattern here was working my way toward a job—a career —that I was passionate about. I had entered a field that made me feel like I was making a difference. I loved working with students, I loved being a student myself (I would continue to take classes over the years, too), and I loved living on campus.

Until I didn't. In the '90s and 2000s, college housing became a lot more "high touch." Remember when I told you about "behind closed doors"? In 1989, my first full year as an RA, you were the "lucky loser" if you landed the suicidal ideation scenario. Everyone was frightened of that role-playing scenario because it was by far the most difficult and sensitive situation that you may have faced as a resident advisor. In the '80's and '90s. These days... you're the lucky loser if you get the active shooter scenario. It's not that the issues got more difficult, but we had to pay much closer attention to them to stop them.

So, while I was in a field I felt drawn to, I was slowly letting the air out of my self-care balloon and becoming something I didn't want to be. An enforcer, emergency services worker, and adjudicator of policy violations.

From 1992 until about 2010, I saw between two and three movies every weekend. Sometimes more. It was a notorious theater jumper. And all this time I'd been telling myself that I loved the cinema... which I am still convinced that I do. But

I think I spent all that time at the movies because I needed to escape a field I didn't believe in any longer.

In 2013 I left my final housing job and took a new position at a community college foundation where I work to this day. It's a fundraising organization for the college—but the best way to describe my current position in Operations and Programs, is "the fundraisers raise the money, and then I spend it." I'm in charge of scholarships, grants, and other activities for the department so our executive director can be out in the community raising money.

And I LOVE THIS JOB! I do. I'm still at a college campus, which is amazing. I get so much energy from academia and the pursuit of higher learning. I still get to work directly with students, because I give away money. I work with amazing women and pretty much have the best boss I've EVER had in my entire career. And I've had some pretty amazing bosses (and some shitty ones too. Well, just two shitty ones).

It's at this point where you are probably saying... so why the side hustles?

Money. That's it. Just money (I shared that in the beginning, remember?).

When I got married I became a total fiscal fiasco. I filed for bankruptcy twice. I've been in more than four debt-management programs. I've been served papers for being sued by my creditors. And more. Thank God for caller ID because I stopped answering the phone for a while. Enter those side hustles like Mary Kay and The Body Shop. I once took a second job in retail. I have done mystery shopping. And while I'm still somewhat of a fiscal fiasco, I have managed to save $1,000 and pay off my car loan just this year.

* * *

When I got married I became a total fiscal fiasco. I filed for bankruptcy twice. I've been in more than four debt-management programs. I've been served papers for being sued by my creditors. And more. Thank God for caller ID because I stopped answering the phone for a while. Enter those side hustles like Mary Kay and The Body Shop. I once took a second job in retail. I have done mystery shopping. And while I'm still somewhat of a fiscal fiasco, I have managed to save $1,000 and pay off my car loan just this year.

(Don't forget—this is not a money mindset book either, because I am not that person.)

This is a book about time management. Priorities. Work-life balance. Drilling down into the things you love and making money from it. Developing a shit ton of additional skill sets that start to overflow into your day job (well, at least for me it did. One of the best parts of this story!). And for me, it finally meant finding a project that I could do with my husband on OUR terms. Which has been hard, but I wouldn't trade any of it. NOT. ONE. SECOND.

See, I'm not one of those side hustlers who wants to quit their day job. I love my day job. And I fully intend to retire from my day job. The side hustle allows me to put passion and attention into other things that matter to me. Swimming. Helping others learn to swim. Career change. Time management and work-life balance.

I still love to see movies. And I love TV, too. But those are treats now. Things that I prioritize for downtime when I want it. Do I get tired? Sure, everyone does. Do I want to take a weekend off sometimes? Naturally! I take vacations from ALL my jobs. But I always look forward to coming back and that's what I love about the vocation and side hustles that I've chosen.

* * *

This book is not a "how to quit your day job" tutorial. And it's not for those folks trying to discover their side hustle. If you're ready to start your side hustle, keep your day job, and balance it all, then you are doing to love, love, love this book. Or if you are looking for a guide on how to double down on time management before you start a side hustle, keep going. There are tons of other books out there that will help you DISCOVER your side hustle and/or get you ready to leave your day job and work for yourself forever.

SO, if you're bootylicious and you think you can handle this, then welcome. I'm glad you're here. We are going to have a lot of fun together. You're probably going to curse me once or twice during this book. You may even tell me I'm full of shit. But if you stick with me and ride it out, you'll be ready to take on the world with your side hustle while still kicking ass at your day job. Hell yes, you are.

And before we go too far into this journey together, I do want to take one more moment to acknowledge that this book has been written in the early aftermath of the COVID-19 pandemic that took hold of the United States around March of 2020 and continues. Much of what I share here came out of the pre-COVID experience, but some lessons and tips derived from the current reality as of July 2020. Much as there was Major League Baseball before and after steroids, there is life as we know it before and after COVID-19. And that's all I'm gonna say about that.

BEFORE WE DIG IN...

I love reflection, journaling, and looking at how our learning truly impacts us. So if you dig that as well, please enjoy the various reflection questions/ journal prompts that will be featured at the end of every chapter. Starting now…

- Now that you know who this book is for… why do you think you need it?
- Think back to why you took your first job… second job… current job? What do you like about it?
- What's the one area of this book which excites you the most?

Elevate Your 8
(Where It Came From, What it is, How it Works)

Going back to my housing days, the line between work and play was hazy at best, especially during the years when I lived where I worked. As I moved up in the field, I need to draw those lines a little thicker and enforce their placement. That was not easy at all. But in pursuing that goal, I learned a great deal about time management and productivity. And I wrote my first two books, Making 'Work' Work for You and Elevate Your 8.

Elevate Your 8 is a productivity philosophy that divides your day into three areas: work, sleep, and "everything else." Twenty-four hours. Three chunks, eight hours each. If we are honoring our work/life balance, we're working just eight hours a day. If we're honoring our health and wellness, we're sleeping eight hours a night. Elevating those other eight hours by prioritization and planning gets us where we need to be to live a full and productive life.

I developed my philosophy shortly after changing careers but before I officially started a business. And Elevate Your 8 has been the main key to having any sort of success—for me—with running the balance between a day job I love and two side hustles I also love. I learned the hard way that you cannot combine your vocations—there are both ethical and rational reasons why that's a bad idea. And we will get into that during a later segment. But for now, here's an introduction to the Elevate Your 8 philosophy and lifestyle.

But before we get started, I want to let you know that there are working hyperlinks throughout this book that contain resources that will help you very much in adopting this philosophy for your day job/side hustle balance. And shoot, if I can make this work, anyone can. The links will send you to various worksheets and planning documents on my website, www.krismcpeak.com/elevate8book. You can do the work without these resources, but it will be much more fun and productive with them. Are you ready?

SLEEP

We need to sleep every night. Good, solid sleep. Sleep that rests our bodies and our minds. Sleep assists our memory. It curbs your appetite. It helps us live longer and decreases the risk of certain diseases.

James Clear of Atomic Habits fame has been writing about sleep for years. In one of his earlier blog posts, he has this to say about sleep:

*"The first purpose of sleep is **restoration**. Every day, your brain accumulates metabolic waste as it goes about*

its normal neural activities. While this is completely normal, too much accumulation of these waste products has been linked to neurological disorders such as Alzheimer's disease.

Alright, so how do we get rid of metabolic waste? Recent research has suggested that sleep plays a crucial role in cleaning out the brain each night. While these toxins can be flushed out during waking hours, researchers have found that clearance during sleep is as much as two-fold faster than during waking hours.

The way this process occurs is fairly remarkable:

During sleep, brain cells shrink by 60 percent, allowing the brain's waste-removal system — called the glymphatic system — to essentially "take out the trash" more easily. The result? Your brain is restored during sleep, and you wake up refreshed and with a clear mind.

The second purpose of sleep is **memory consolidation.**

Sleep is crucial for memory consolidation, which is the process that maintains and strengthens your long-term memories. Insufficient or fragmented sleep can hamper your ability to form both concrete memories (facts and figures) and emotional memories.

*Finally, sleep is paramount for **metabolic health**. Studies have shown that when you sleep 5.5 hours per night instead of 8.5 hours per night, a lower proportion of the energy you burn comes from fat, while more comes from carbohydrates and protein. This can predispose you to fat gain and muscle loss. Additionally, insufficient sleep or abnormal sleep cycles can lead to insulin insensitivity and metabolic syndrome, increasing your risk of diabetes and heart disease.*

All of this to say, that better sleep is critical for your mental and physical health."

Then are scientific theories that hope to explain

why we sleep and why we NEED sleep. Healthy Sleep from the Harvard Medical School outlines several of these on their website.

There is the **Inactivity Theory**—suggesting that "inactivity at night is an adaptation that served a survival function by keeping organisms out of harm's way at times when they would be particularly vulnerable." So, don't move and stay away from the dark so you don't get eaten.

Next up is the **Energy Conservation Theory,** suggesting "the primary function of sleep is to reduce an individual's energy demand and expenditure during part of the day or night, especially at times when it is least efficient to search for food." Our body temperature and caloric demand are reduced when we sleep, which supports the notion that we need to sleep to conserve our energy resources.

* * *

The **Restorative Theory** maintains that "sleep provides an opportunity for the body to repair and rejuvenate itself." Some studies prove that necessary body functions like muscle growth, tissue repair, and protein synthesis occur mostly during sleep.

A recent theory has to do with changes in the structure and organization of the brain—this is known as **Brain Plasticity Theory**. While not entirely understood, it is becoming clearer that sleep plays a critical role in the brain development of infants and young children.

With all this science backing up the importance of sleep... why do so many people deprive themselves? There are MANY, many reasons. But what I hear, over and over again... wait for it... **"I don't have time."**

We think that we don't have enough hours in the

day to get things done. Because we are overworked anyway and can't embrace better work and life alignment, we force ourselves to stay up late or get up early to get things done. Some of us completely waste our time with social media, television, and video games. We choose socializing, chores, eating, working our day job, and time-wasters over a good night's rest.

I once knit an entire scarf in one night while watching two Billy Wilder movies. On a work night. Why I did this I'll never understand. I didn't even wear a scarf the next day. But I guess I wanted to finish it. And it was only the tenth time I'd watched *Witness for the Prosecution* in about two weeks (maybe it was the movies. I love Billy Wilder's films). It was a great scarf and all, but I could have watched the movie another time, and I definitely could have completed the knitting project the next day. I have no excuses.

* * *

We may be so stressed, sick, and overly medicated that our eight hours of sleep are not quality hours. And this defeats the purpose of sleep. According to Dr. Annise Wilson, assistant professor of neurology and of pulmonary, critical care and sleep medicine at Baylor University, "High levels of stress impair sleep by prolonging how long it takes to fall asleep and fragmenting sleep. Sleep loss triggers our body's stress response system, leading to an elevation in stress hormones, namely cortisol, which further disrupts sleep," Wilson explained. "Research has shown that sleep plays an important role in learning and memory. Chronic sleep deprivation also has been associated with decreased metabolism and endocrine dysfunction. "

Our medications can also play a role in disrupting sleep. Once again, the Sleep Foundation states the following about certain medications and how they impact your blissful slumber:

* * *

Medications That Cause Insomnia

Drugs that treat heart problems and blood pressure can cause sleeplessness, as can certain antidepressants, thyroid medications, decongestants, and some herbal medications. Other drugs contain chemicals that act as stimulants, which can also keep you up at night. These include ADHD medications, asthma medications, anti-smoking medications, and some pain killers that contain caffeine.

Medications That Disrupt Sleep

Some drugs don't interfere with falling asleep, but can still affect sleep quality. For instance, beta-blockers used for high blood pressure and some cholesterol-lowering drugs may cause nightmares and nighttime waking. Certain cough medications can also lower sleep quality by suppressing REM sleep.

Medications That Make You Drowsy

On the flip side, certain drugs lead to daytime drowsiness, which can also disrupt your sleep patterns. For instance, many cold and allergy medicines cause sleepiness during the day. Some antidepressants and anti-anxiety medications can make you feel sluggish. Other drowsiness-related drugs include opioid pain medication, muscle relaxants, beta-blockers for blood pressure, and anticonvulsants used to treat seizures.

There are a plethora of resources out there for how to improve your sleep, and my favorite one is the book Sleep Smarter by Shawn Stevenson. I will quote this resource often through this chapter. His book is useful, funny, contemporary, uses science to make points and pop culture to drive those points home. I chose to purchase the Audible version of his book since Shawn reads his work as well. Beyond what you will learn in this chapter, I highly recommend getting your hands on this book. You will not be sorry.

Through all my research I learned that there are several easy things we can do to take back our nights and get better sleep. Even just instituting one or two of these recommendations can move you closer to fulfilling the first chunk of this philosophy: fall back in love with sleep!

Reduce Caffeine

Caffeine is a stimulant and can prevent you from getting a good night's rest. It is found in coffee, tea, soda, some candies, and some weird places like yogurt and protein bars. I'd been taught as a young adult that eating plain M&Ms can provide a good shot of caffeine if you are traveling on the road and need to stay awake. I'd also been told that Mountain Dew has the most caffeine of any other carbonated beverage. All I know is, when I have more than one cup of coffee in the morning,

I'm jittery for a while. If I have a Diet Coke with dinner, I'll have a hard time getting to sleep.

So who's old enough to remember No-Doz or Vivarin? When I was a resident advisor in college, we used to get "good stuff" boxes at the beginning of the school year. They were filled with amazing samples and full-size products like shaving cream, deodorant, tampons, condoms, snacks, and VIVARIN. I only pulled an all-nighter one time during my five-year undergraduate pursuit which was the only time I ever tried Vivarin. It was a big mistake. Huge. I felt horrible for days. So that's all I have to say about that.

According to Sleep Education, the average daily consumption of caffeine by adults in the US is about 300 mg per person. This is about three times higher than the world average. No wonder we have issues sleeping. Between coffee shops, soda and energy drinks, and those plain M&Ms, this stimulant is everywhere.

The website from Sleep Education goes on to say, "Caffeine begins to affect your body very quickly. It reaches a peak level in your blood within 30 to 60 minutes. It has a half-life of 3 to 5 hours. The half-life is the time it takes your body to eliminate half the drug. The remaining caffeine can stay in your body for a long time." Dang—no wonder that Diet Coke nags me if I have it at dinner (or lunch for that matter). To keep caffeine from disrupting your sleep, try not to have any caffeinated beverages after two or three p.m.

Carey Lawson, an executive director of advancement from Eunice, Louisiana, attributes eliminating caffeine at three p.m. to her sleep wins. And my buddy Phoebe Chiang, a Los Angeles based event planner, knocks off the caffeine by four p.m. so she can be ready for bed after nine p.m.

* * *

Other Beverages?

While some people do pass out after consuming too much to drink or paying hard, alcohol is generally not something that can help you sleep. And yet twenty percent of Americans rely on alcohol as their main sleep aid.

The Sleep Doctor website states, "In the body, alcohol disrupts circadian functioning, directly interfering with the ability of the master biological clock to synchronize itself. Because circadian rhythms have such a powerful, dominating influence over the way our bodies function, the disruptive effects of alcohol can be widespread, affecting sleep and other systems."

A 2013 article in Psychology Today states, "Alcohol consumption, in excess or too close to bedtime, diminishes the quality of sleep, often leads to more waking throughout the night and lessens the time spent in REM sleep and slow-wave sleep in the latter part of the night, the deepest and most restorative phase of sleep." Alcohol is considered a depressant, but the immediate effects of alcohol can act as a stimulant —this is called biphasic effects. According to this same article, "Many people continue to believe that alcohol helps them sleep and have a few drinks as a 'nightcap' before bed. It is easy to see why people might believe this. It is, after all, a fairly common experience for people to become sleepy after having a few drinks. A 'few more' and they might even pass out. This is because alcohol has a biphasic effect on sleep and arousal. This makes it difficult to be aware of the negative effects because the positive ones come first and are more obvious." That's kinda like how I'm gonna feel later if I eat that milkshake now, right?

To engage in a better night's rest, cease your alcohol consumption at dinner, and don't drink too much before bed.

Reduce Your Evening Entertainment—Or at Least Change It

I used to be one of those people who "absolutely needed" the TV on to go to sleep. What this wound up doing for me was waking me up in the middle of the night, noticing that I didn't like what was on the tube and changing channels. And that usually meant investing thirty or so minutes into whatever I chose. But even if you have no television in your bedroom, even checking out that new episode of whatever hot show you love before bed can keep you awake. The Huffington Post cited an article that states sixty-eight percent of participants watched TV for more than fifty-five minutes in the two hours leading up to bedtime—precious minutes that could be spent sleeping. To minimize TV interference, DVR or stream your must-see shows and tune in earlier in the evening or on weekends.

* * *

This next study might explain a little bit of your weight gain if you are an evening TV watcher. Health.com shared a study published in JAMA Internal Medicine that found that sleeping with the TV on in your bedroom "may be a risk factor for weight gain, overweight, and obesity." The authors of the report analyzed data from more than forty-three thousand women for the study. They went so far as to say that reducing your exposure to artificial light at night could "be a useful intervention for obesity prevention."

So reading is better than television before bed, right? Not necessarily. Engaging in novels or stories that are scary, overly emotional, or high energy can raise your blood pressure and heart rate, which makes it harder to sleep. Eva Kennedy, a higher-education administrator in the San Fernando Valley, makes sure she turns off her television early and reads in her living room while listening to what she calls "good music." Depending on the day and her mood, this could be soft country music or classical music. And most of the time, the music she chooses has limited songs, "so I normally fall asleep before all the songs are done." Good work, Eva.

Your Phone

Uh, yeah, I'm going there even though I wanted to avoid this. Because I am quite certainly one of the worst culprits (now that you know that you should feel free to email me at info@krismcpeak.com and ask me how I'm doing in this arena. Thank you).

Mobile phones are the world's biggest blessing and curse. On the one hand, we can be so much more productive using our phones because of all the handy dandy apps and gadgets… but there are many scientists and medical folks who believe that phones do not belong in the bedroom.

* * *

An article in USA Today states, "To fall asleep, your body needs an increase in a hormone called melatonin. Problem is, a backlit phone or tablet decreases melatonin production." This can lead to some tossing and turning in the bedroom. If you are an iPhone user, then you know that Apple introduced the Night Shift feature on their phones, which reduces the backlit blue lights to a warmer tone that can reduce the disruptions. There are also glasses you can purchase that will reduce the amount the blue light your eyeballs are taking in. I have a super fun pair that I got from my FabFitFun subscription; and they are quite stylish in addition to being functional and helpful!

There is also a major concern with the radiation emitted by wireless phones and their antennas. The National Cancer Institute has an entire fact sheet dedicated to this. Some of the details include, "Cell phones emit radio frequency energy (radio waves), a form of non-ionizing radiation, from their antennas. Tissues nearest to the antenna can absorb this energy." If you are concerned about this, read articles, and look for other places to store your mobile phone at night. I was fortunate enough two years ago to attend a retreat where were asked—expected—to turn off our cell phones and tablets during the sessions. It was quite liberating to know that I didn't have to have my phone on and in my hands constantly. And I also learned at this retreat about alarm clocks that simulate the sunrise according to your sleep and wake schedule. So I bought one. And I love it. You set your wake time and choose from several "waking" tones; then the clock will start to light up thirty minutes before your wakeup time. This is meant to wake you gradually and comfortably. It's awesome. I can even change the color of the light simulation. Love, love, love my alarm clock!

Bedroom Conditions

The National Sleep Foundation has some amazing resources on sleeping disorders and other sleep-related topics. Their "Inside the Bedroom" section of their website is quite useful.

For example—how many times have you awoken in the middle of the night and had night sweats or were otherwise uncomfortably warm? That's because our body temperature can be affected by warmer temperatures. NSF recommends a bedroom temperature of around sixty-five degrees for optimal sleep. That sounds cold, doesn't it? But as someone who loves to snuggle up under the blankets at night with my hubby and dog, I love it. And it works! But if you or your significant other find that temperature to be too cold, there are bed liners you can purchase that will keep your body temperature from getting out of control while you sleep.

* * *

Light and darkness affect our sleep. Too much light makes your body think it's still daytime; you should be up and mobile. Our body needs a dark room to relax into sleep. This is one of the reasons why shift work is so awful for humans—for night-shift workers to get the best possible sleep, one has to blacken out the windows and doors to keep the room dark. In Shawn Stevenson's book that I referenced earlier, he shares that shift work has been classified by the American Cancer Association as a 2A type carcinogen, grouped with nitrates, nitrites, anabolic sterols, lead compounds, and the consumption of red meat... along with one of the longest list of chemicals I've seen in a long time and I am not going to type them all to even to beef up my word count (ha ha).

Artificial light at night can also trigger the brain's production of melatonin, making it harder to fall asleep and stay asleep. I've started lighting candles in our house in the living room about two hours before bedtime so that we can still see to walk around the house, but we don't have to have too much light on in the house that could disrupt our sleep later (although, not the summer months). Plus it makes the house smell good. A luscious bonus.

Changing your sheets is just as much about sleep quality as it is about hygiene. The smell of fresh sheets is pleasing and can aid in our sleep quality. The National Sleep Foundation recommends washing your sheets once a week, and sprinkling baking soda on sheets and mattress covers, then vacuuming. Choose laundry detergent with a pleasing scent and make sure you aren't allergic to it.

In Sleep Smarter, Shawn Stevenson dedicates an entire chapter to creating your sleep sanctuary. He suggests things like blackout curtains, house plans, and removing all devices from the bedroom. And then... Shawn says to use that bedroom only for sleep and sex. And I think I can live with that.

Exercise

"I'm not a morning person" is the reason I hear most often on why my friends and colleagues don't work out in the morning. Many of them are runners or gym rats. With the advent of twenty-four-hour fitness facilities, we can stretch our days to the point where we are hitting up the elliptical at two-thirty a.m.

And this practice is no good for us. First of all, if your adrenaline from a workout is up and charging, it's going to be a while before your body wants to go to sleep. Secondly, remember that our bodies were not engineered to be up twenty-four hours a day. So when it's dark outside, we should be sleeping. Which is why the energy you get from either an early morning workout lunchtime workout is the best for maintaining a solid, regular sleep schedule? The energy and metabolism boost you get through the day and allow your body temperature to get back where it's supposed to for sleep.

My friend and fellow swimmer Heidi Sheaks, owner and stylist at West Coast Cuts and Colors of Woodland Hills (you'll hear from her again, she's one of my favorite people), says that swimming every morning before work ensures that she gets a good night's sleep. "I used to be an insomniac," Sheaks states. "I did not realize that a daily routine of morning swim exercise not only helps me sustain the workday, but I find I can fall asleep at night."

A study by Kelly Glazer Baron from Northwestern University agrees with her. While other forms of exercise can stress our bodies, "Swimming can break that cycle both mentally and physically. Sensory deprivation, a complete lack of stress on the body, stretching, fat burning, muscle building, weight loss, combating depression, all of these powerful aspects of swimming are sure to help you sleep more soundly."

Hormones

This realization came only recently when I made my first trip to see a functional medicine/holistic doctor. You know, menopause and crap like that. Trying to eat better and figure out why my system was all messed up even though I haven't had my period in a few years (sorry, fellas).

This doctor—who I just love, by the way—had me take a bunch of different tests to explore some things. We were looking for why my energy was low and I wasn't motivated to work out as well as why I was still super cranky to be around sometimes. I took a food sensitivity test, did a whole crapload of new blood work, and a hormone test. The latter of the three was the most fascinating since I had to do daily mouth swabs—six of them—and that determined when all my various hormone levels were functioning (or not functioning, as the case was). My cortisol in the morning was low and it was determined that I was having some adrenal fatigue. My doctor can explain it much better, but I've found some additional resources for you.

According to Dr. Michael Breus (the Sleep Doctor), there's this thing called an HPA axis, which is short for the hypothalamic-pituitary-adrenal axis. This nifty axis thingamabob combines parts of the central nervous and endocrine systems. Cortisol is produced in the adrenal glands, and the hypothalamus and pituitary gland, located in the brain, monitor cortisol levels and send messages to the adrenal system to adjust its production, depending on the body's needs and circumstances. It's the complex, dynamic communication of the HPA axis that produces cortisol and helps to regulate body functions ranging from sleep-wake cycles to stress and mood to digestion and immune function.

Like nearly all hormones in the human body, cortisol has a daily, twenty-four-hour rhythm. For most biotypes, cortisol levels are at their highest in the morning, usually around nine a.m. Cortisol begins to rise gradually in the second half of a night's sleep. The hormone begins a more rapid rise around the time you're waking up before peaking at about nine. From that point on, cortisol makes a gradual decline throughout the day, reaching its lowest levels around midnight. The activity of the HPA axis, which produces cortisol, reduces to its lowest levels in the evenings, right around your bedtime. In this way, cortisol plays a critical role in sleep-wake cycles: stimulating wakefulness in the morning, continuing to support alertness throughout the day while gradually dropping to allow the body's own internal sleep drive and other hormones—including adenosine and melatonin—to rise, and help bring about sleep.

New Parents

While I'm not a parent, I've heard the stories. "How much sleep are you getting these days?" For new parents, figuring out the sleep schedule so the newborn gets all his or her due attention can be tricky. Stephanie Hilten, director of advancement for Carl Sandburg College, has a set system for tending to their newborn at home with her husband. She states, "Since we are opposites—he is a night owl and I'm an early bird—after we complete whatever household chores that need to be finished after dinner, he plays Xbox and I go to sleep… usually around eight or nine or ten. Then he lets me sleep until eleven and watches our son sleep on the baby monitor while he plays Xbox.

This allows me time to get a few good hours before we move our son into our room and he comes to bed. It works for us because we both get whatever hours we need and still sleep in bed together, something we believe is important in our marriage." So there is an argument for X-Box... for new parents.

Insomnia

Insomnia is a common sleep disorder that makes it hard for you to fall asleep or stay asleep. It leads to daytime sleepiness and not feeling rested or refreshed when you wake up. Approximately fifty percent of adults experience occasional insomnia. One in ten people reports having chronic insomnia.

Yes—there are several types of insomnia, which I learned all about on The Sleep Foundation website. Here are the five specific types:

Acute insomnia

A brief episode of difficulty sleeping. Acute insomnia is usually caused by a life event, such as a stressful change in a person's job, receiving bad news, or travel. Often acute insomnia resolves without any treatment.

Chronic insomnia

A long-term pattern of difficulty sleeping. Insomnia is usually considered chronic if a person has trouble falling asleep or staying asleep at least three nights per week for three months or longer. Some people with chronic insomnia have a long-standing history of difficulty sleeping. Chronic insomnia has many causes.

Comorbid insomnia

Insomnia occurs with another condition. Psychiatric symptoms—such as anxiety and depression—are known to be associated with changes in sleep. Certain medical conditions can either cause insomnia or make a person uncomfortable at night (as in the case of arthritis or back pain, which may make it hard to sleep).

Onset insomnia
Difficulty falling asleep at the beginning of the night.

Maintenance insomnia
The inability to stay asleep. People with maintenance insomnia wake up during the night and have difficulty returning to sleep.

Healthline.com reports that the causes of your insomnia will depend on the type of sleeplessness you experience. Acute insomnia may be caused by stress, an upsetting or traumatic event, or changes to your sleep habits.
Chronic insomnia lasts for at least three months

and is usually secondary to another problem or a combination of problems, including medical conditions (arthritis or back pain), psychological issues (anxiety or depression), or substance abuse.

Listen up—sleep is nothing to overlook when it comes to your health and wellness. That is what makes it such an important part of the Elevate Your 8 Philosophy and why I say, "honor your health and wellness by sleeping eight hours every night." And as we learned in this section of the book, you need to pay close attention to how you approach your nightly sleep to make it the healthiest sleep possible.

Now that we've awakened to a new day after an amazing night of sleep, let's go to work…

WORK

Unless you were born into money, or you won the

lottery, or you're like Jules in Pulp Fiction (you're gonna "walk the earth," like Kane in Kung Fu)—chances are you have to go to a day job to support yourself and your family.

The blog Trans4Mind discusses several differences between your job and your vocation. Job isn't always liked. You have predefined working hours and a set wage. Jobs don't always align with your values. And you will eventually be fired, quit, or leave your job.

Vocations, on the other hand, are defined as callings. Your vocation means you are doing things just right and you are in the field that fuels your passion. You will never truly "retire" from your vocation. You enjoy your weekends and anticipate the beauty that is Monday when you return to your calling. You feel happy all the time because your work is a natural expression of YOU.

* * *

What sounds better?

In my first book, Making 'Work' Work for You, I outline several strategies and hacks to help you manage your job should you be struggling. The book's sections are divided according to my experiences through twenty-plus years of work in higher education. I don't want to duplicate that book here—that would be silly. But I will highlight a few things you can think about when it comes to those eight hours every day when you physically go to a place of employment and earn your living.

Generational Differences

I fully identify with my Gen X self and I value work/life balance and flexibility above all other values my workday. Most of my former supervisors were Baby Boomers; my parents were of the Greatest Generation. My father in particular taught me about persistence and dedication, but he also encouraged me to live life to the fullest. A former Boomer supervisor told me that working forty hours a week in my current position was unrealistic. I've had supervisors remind me to take a vacation while others turned my requests down and judged my requests as not being "reasonable." Who takes a vacation to go to a film festival anyway?

Boomers focused greatly on loyalty and putting in the hours to get ahead. A 2006 article in the Chicago Tribune states, "For them, the best way to achieve was to become the workaholic generation." Which at times made things very difficult for us Gen Xers who were ready to go to happy hour or hit the gym. I mostly bring this up to remind you that generational differences do affect us in the workplace. If you think your values are being challenged by a supervisor of a different generation, talk to her. Tell her your thoughts or concerns. Try to negotiate a middle ground—but don't be pushy. Remember that you bought this book because you want to keep that nine to five while you rock your side hustle. Wanna change jobs? That's a different book.

How Did I Get Here?

Not all of us knew what we wanted to do right out of high school, or even right out of college. Many of us fell into our professions because of some involvement we had in college. That's exactly how I found myself working in higher education. In college, I was a resident advisor in the residence hall for two and a half years. When I realized I could get paid real money to do this for a living, I geeked out. I can make donations and plan parties and get paid for it? Yes, I'm in.

Since then, my path has been rough at times, but still rewarding. And there finally came a time where residence hall work wasn't good for me anymore. I switched to another field in higher education, one that is very different from college housing. And I'm happier than a pig in slop these days. I still make a huge difference in the lives of students, but I have forged a path that lets me go home at four-thirty p.m. and enjoy most of my weekends to myself instead of those taking calls at three-thirty a.m., etc.

You may have a similar story—a job in high school or college led to a career once you received the proper training. Or maybe you found a job that was exciting when you were twenty-four, but there were not enough opportunities for advancement. Therefore, you've been on a lateral path ever since then. Even worse—you took a job because it came with a regular paycheck and now you curse that decision on a daily—God forbid—even hourly basis. But whether you thank the universe for landing you in the right place or biff yourself on the head a la Special Agent Jethro Gibbs because of your foolish decision, all of us challenge our vocation from time to time. This is not only normal, it's healthy. Life events, relationships, and all sorts of outside factors can affect our daily nine to five, even when we do our best to shelter them from each other.

But you should be honest with yourself. Yeah, you gotta make a living; but according to Dolly Parton, you gotta make a living, too. Don't let yourself suffer in a position that is slowly sucking the life out of you or driving you to drink. If that's you— you may want to put this book down and pick up Making 'Work' Work for You, or check out my online course, "Home by 5 - How to Thrive in Your Dream Job and Achieve Time Freedom."

Tricks for Getting Through...

Picture this: you've decided to gut out another year at your current gig... or, it's just absolutely the busiest season for you and your colleagues, and you find yourself grasping at straws, sleeping poorly, and eating crap. You need some tips and tricks for reimagining your workday. For example —don't let your calendar run amuck over you. Control it. Keep it clean and tidy. Schedule lunch every day and schedule travel time between meetings. Ask your assistant to block project time for you on your calendar—or, better yet, do this yourself. You'll get so much more work done in those work blocks, you'll forget how grumpy you are because of how productive you've been (look to Chapter Two for more tips on this strategy).

Looking at this another way—do you like your supervisor and colleagues, but the work itself is not sustaining your passion? Maybe it's time to have that conversation with your supervisor, let her know that you need a challenge. Ask her if you can take on some more projects, maybe things that align with your talents and strengths (purchase StrengthsFinder 2.0 to learn more about this strengths thing. It's VERY cool).

And damn it, you need to take a vacation! This isn't just some random benefit that HR dangles but hopes you never use. Vacation and time away are crucial for regeneration and further engagement in your place of business. A 2015 article in The Guardian states, "Researchers at Oxford Economics hired by the US Travel Association put the numbers [unused vacation time] at about one hundred sixty-nine days, equivalent to $52.4 billion in lost benefits." That's 211,250 days of vacation left on the table to die. Pathetic. Just pathetic.

But why? Some people want to show their loyalty, and not taking a vacation is a possible way to do that. Another quotation from The Guardian: "We are the only industrial country that does not mandate vacation days, and twenty-five percent of our workers receive none of them at all." Are you freaking kidding me?

* * *

It is, however, a top-down practice. Employees who see their supervisors take vacations are more likely to do the same. So, if you supervise others, take some damn time off, for crying out loud. And if you don't supervise others, be the trailblazer and go on a staycation or vacation. For realz.

Attitude

As Arvind Devalia says on Lifehack.com, "Remember, you are more than your work." Let your soul and spirit define how you approach your job or vocation rather than letting the job define you. Plus, unrealistic expectations on what you "should" be doing in your life (from parents, family, friends, supervisors) can be frustrating.

Devalia also suggests contributing to a productive workspace and a pleasant work environment as much as possible. Don't gossip. Don't carry your dissatisfaction around like a big rock on your shoulders. If your attitude is positive and optimistic, that can be a happy influence on your colleagues and peers. Charles J. Alaimo from Huffington Post so wisely says, "Your perspective will determine your reality." In other words, if you think you have a shitty job, then you have one.

Geoffrey James from Inc.com writes about ways you can improve your attitude at work. Some of these are obvious, but others sort of hit me upside the head. For example, "Use setbacks to improve your skills." Of course! This is how we learn and grow. It doesn't always have to be during our annual review or performance appraisal where we figure out how to improve in our job. Rather than getting defensive when a colleague doesn't like our project idea, ask yourself: "Maybe I could have presented it differently." Or, "I should learn more about her perspective." This also allows you to go within and find any blocks you are having that made you feel negatively in the first place; if you can identify those and just work on yourself, you won't be pointing the finger at the other guy all the time.

Okay, I know what you are thinking. All this stuff about tips and hacks and attitude is great. But it doesn't change the fact that I work twelve hours a day.

- I can't work only eight hours a day.
- I can't get the work done.
- I can't put myself at risk at work.

What is all this "I can't" crap?

Kathy Caprino from Forbes Magazine writes this about overtime and overworking (April 30, 2015):

- *Employees often believe that working longer hours means they'll get more done.*
- *As managers arrive at the office earlier and depart later each day, their employees will mimic their schedules because they believe working long*

hours is necessary to gain approval.

♦ *Employee-fostered culture often dictates that those who work longer hours are going to be promoted more quickly for "working harder."*

♦ *Employers do not effectively communicate work-life expectations, so employees default to prioritizing work over life outside.*

♦ *Finally, managers don't have complete visibility into each employee's workloads, so they continue assigning additional work without considering existing projects and responsibilities.*

If you are a manager, these five points can help you plan and prioritize your day, as well as show how to support your team with their work. As a manager, it's your job to role-model that work/life balance to your team (if you are a manager who doesn't believe in work/life balance, this is probably the wrong book for you. Sorry).

But what if you aren't a manager. How do you tell

your boss that you have too much work or that you "prefer to go home at five p.m. and this is why". For many of us, this can be a daunting and frightening task. We may feel nervous about speaking up; and yet, if no one will advocate for you, you must advocate for yourself.

Kyle Lee from The Muse outlines some great suggestions and I agree with all of them. The bottom line is you have to approach your supervisor with patience and respect and speak from a place of appreciation and honesty.

Problem Solve: to reduce your workload and get back to the eight-hour day, you need to be able to solve programs rather than whining or complaining about said problems. For example, talk about how you can complete this specific report or project in a shorter amount of time and why you believe it can be done. Or, share your ideas on how your staff meeting can be shorter and more productive for everyone. ADD VALUE.

Be Specific: generalizations aren't going to help you here. You have to outline the specific issue and provide a specific solution. You can't just say, "There's too much to do and I don't have time." Instead, say, "My current workload for this quarter, which includes eight financial reports and four evaluations, seems unrealistic with my current meeting schedule." Then propose the solution.

Focus on the Future: you want to be strategically future-oriented because you can't change the past. You will need to provide a resounding argument (not a fight, mind you) on how your future performance will be improved by your recommendations. For starters, "If I could get a fifteen-minute break in the morning and afternoon to get outside and walk around, my head will be much clearer and I can get focused on finishing my project." Or, "if the administrative assistants can all stagger our lunches, there will always be covered at the front desk and no one will have to be stuck here while everyone else is at lunch."

Aaron McCoy from Idealist Careers also suggests leaving emotion out of the conversation, express concerns about quality, and convey your appreciation for the opportunity to share your ideas. You can't be emotional in a situation like this because it decreases your credibility. Your manager may instead decide you shouldn't have the position at all! Sharing how the quality of your work will improve the specific changes you suggest will impress upon your supervisor that you care about creating a sound, quality product. And you must say thank you. Appreciation of the time is important to recognize. Your supervisor may be much, much busier than you are. Treat that opportunity to discuss your concerns as a gift.

Sadly, you might do all this work and provide the

most amazing and convincing reasons why your workload and work hours should be reduced and your boss can still say, "Toughen up." Or, "This is the job you've accepted."

Well poop.

Now what?

That's a situation that will take some additional soul searching beyond the scope of this book. But given that I've been there myself, here are some options:

- **Look for another job**
- **Go back to working the long hours**
- **Work more efficiently at the office than your coworkers**

I constantly go back to this notion. When a proposal was put in front of me as the supervisor or manager and the employee seemed convinced that it could be done, why not give it a try? I feel as though managers need to listen to their employees and treat them as members of a team, not serfs in the kingdom.

I want to deviate from the current conversation and introduce an interesting time management tool that is the office version of the "Four-Way Win" that I described in both of my previous books about weekends.

Jeffrey B. Harrington, MBA, from California State University-Chico, has an incredible strategy for both taking a work break and doing networking. It's what he calls "network naturally." Or, in other words, "leave your desk behind and talk to people." When Jeff was in his first professional position after college, he worked as an assistant hall director at a mid-size California university and developed what he calls a "career leveraging" practice in his day to day work routine. His daily networking walks became a popular skill that he homed in his four years living on campus, and he continued to practice this in his role as an admissions counselor, and now as a career advisor.

To hear Jeff tell this story specifically, check out Episode 003 of The Elevate Your 8 Podcast.

Jeff's tips:

- Physically get out of the office. If you need an excuse to leave your department, go buy some coffee or a snack.
- Go the long way to the bathroom on a different floor and pass the desks of people you don't know well. Genuinely say "hello" as you pass.
- Personally hand-deliver something to a colleague's office that doesn't need to be hand-delivered.
- Stop by a neighboring office instead of writing ten emails back and forth to solve a problem. People appreciate the effort.

* * *

THAT is the Elevate Your 8 Philosophy as defined by the book and the podcast that followed. The podcast is still live and you can check it out anywhere podcasts are played. I would LOVE for you to leave a rating and review, should you take a minute to check it out.

Meanwhile, we are ready to move on to finding balance in our day job search and our side hustles. These next two chapters go a little deeper into some of the areas discussed in this chapter on "Elevate Your 8." But if you want to take your productivity to the next level before jumping into the balance world, then here is how you can move towards completing the Elevate Your 8 Challenge.

Go to krismcpeak.com/elevate8book and download all the supporting materials.

◆ Choose a start date for your twenty-one-day experiment.

- Sign the pledge.
- Spend seven days on the sleep journal and then another seven days on the Time on Task —but do not do both at once.
- Journal for a couple of days on your findings (because this is science, bitches!) and come to conclusions on what needs to change in your life to truly Elevate Your 8.

DIGGING DEEP...

- What are your initial thoughts on "Elevate Your 8?"
- Which of the tips in the "Sleep" or "Work" section sound most interesting to you and why?
- Will you be taking the twenty-one-day challenge? Why or why not?
- What other time management processes have worked for you in the past? Why do you enjoy them?

Balance at the Day Job

"Okay, McPeak, I get all this Elevate Your 8 stuff... but how does that change things in my day job?"

Yes, good question.

The biggest reason I hear from my friends and colleagues about why they don't have side hustles and/or spend time on their hobbies is... wait for it....

I DON'T HAVE TIME.

And if you've paid attention to anything I've said so far you know that we all have the same amount of time as anyone else does.

We just don't MAKE the time or USE the time effectively.

* * *

Which is what Elevate Your 8 is all about... but more importantly... it's why people aren't living a full life and enjoying their day jobs.

So to make this work we've got to make more sense of how we use our time in our day job.

SCHEDULING

Have you heard the phrase, "control your calendar or it will control you?" It is one of the truest truisms that I know in this world. In my previous life as a housing professional, especially in middle and upper management, my day was spent drawing in meetings. Meeting after meeting after meeting. I spent so much time in meetings that I didn't have time to DO my job—and, of course, that's a big reason why so many people work such long hours. They don't have time to work because some blowhole thinks that their time is better spent in meetings talking about working.

Now, I realize that was kind of harsh. That blowhole might be you. Or it might be the very best boss you've ever had, who just happens to have a serious hard-on for meetings.

So how do we fix this?

We don't provide the availability for meetings. Because we manage our calendar and we schedule a time for work.

I did not invent this concept. F. John Reh, Tony Robbins, and Shawn Stevenson have written about "chunking" before. My secret is to make appointments with myself and tell myself ahead of time what I'm going to be doing.

Here's an example: I know that I'm the most

creative and energetic in the earlier parts of the day—which is why a morning routine works so well for me. So when I consider the biggest projects I need to complete for the day, week, or month, I'm going to carve time to work on it in the morning hours. That's an appointment with me. Using your calendar app of choice, do the following.

Name of Meeting: Work Time
Location: Content Calendar, Clean Up Email Box, Return Voicemail
Time: 9 a.m. – 11 a.m.

Ta-da! I've just scheduled in my three biggest things for the day into a two-hour block that's being held just for me. And because I'm a director, I can get away with "Work Time" as the name of a meeting. My boss was so impressed with this that she got her assistant helping her try it out now and then (because, dang, that woman is in a shit ton of meetings!).

But what if your boss is a little vary of you scheduling "work time" and not making yourself available for meetings? I've got two thoughts for that:

◆ Tell your supervisor that you are most productive during this part of the day and you want to focus that time and energy on the most pressing tasks for the week.

◆ Make up a phony person with whom you have a standing meeting (unless your supervisor is a super-duper busybody, he or she won't have the time to notice that you're just doing work and being damn productive, too!).

Yup, I've used both of these tactics and they work. Especially the first one. Unless your supervisor is a super-duper micromanager or completely dense, this is an argument that you may very well win due to the common sense of it all.

Meanwhile, you've still got colleagues and other work connections who are probably going to want some of your time now and then. In this case, try your darnedest to schedule standing meetings one hour before your lunch break or one hour after your lunch break.

If you are like me and you prefer a set lunchtime every day (see the section on workday routines), then scheduling a standing meeting one hour before lunch accomplishes several things. First, it gives that group a set period to get things done. And secondly, no one likes to drag meetings into lunch, so your colleagues will likely be more like you and want to finish what needs to be done and get on with the day.

Whether you are leading the meeting or just

contributing, you can role-model the type of behavior that helps moves things along and holds the hour sacred so everyone can get in and done. Suggest that the "reporting" function of the meeting be replaced by short written reports that people are encouraged to read before the meeting. Or do a "whip around" that's limited to one to two minutes per person to cover the most important thing. Cover "old business" first and limit it to five to ten minutes. If the group can't find consensus on the issues, then table it to the next meeting. Cover "new business" next and give it the proper time it needs, but end the discussion five to seven minutes before the end of the meeting. Use that time to recap and determine the set action items for the next meeting. Then close it up and get to your lunch. Bang, done!

Ad-hoc meetings or special meetings can be scheduled after lunch, particularly if you are NOT the one calling or leading the meeting. After lunch is usually the time of day when the "lull" begins, so if you are placed in a situation where you absolutely MUST be present, you'll give it your all and the time will just breeze by.

I fully realize that this is not a "given" in any way, shape, or form. But there are things you can do to stay energized after lunch and make that meeting incredibly productive for everyone involved. First, have the meeting in a space other than yours. A building across campus, a different floor, even a separate conference room in your regular office space... but go somewhere that requires you to walk a little. You may need to end your lunch early to get there on time, but consider that walk the mid-day exercise break that you'll create for yourself (more on that later). Have a full water bottle in hand and your note-taking pad or device. Continuing to consume water will keep you hydrated and present; and then you'll have to go to the bathroom when the meeting is coming to a close, so you'll have to be excused to use the facilities before you return to your own space. And always schedule buffer or travel time for yourself so you aren't feeling rushed or giving up sacred time that's needed for something else.

Another way of controlling your calendar—and this is particularly useful if you have an assistant or someone in the office who monitors your calendar for you—limit yourself to three meetings per day. My supervisor does this and it has not only kept her sanity during busy times, but it also requires that I be prepared. The day that I want to meet might be on a day that's already full, and I am asked to take an earlier slot. OR it may be that I can't get to see her for a full week and then I have time to schedule the work time related to that meeting effectively.

PRODUCTIVITY

Okay, you've got your calendar under control and

you have some excellent tactics for keeping your day on schedule. Look at all at the work time you've created for yourself! I am so proud of you for taking that first step.

But now you've got to produce and that means you need to have productive work sessions for yourself. That requires a bit more discipline plus ranking the most important things for the day. AND holding yourself accountable.

At the time of this writing, I am participating in a time management masterclass led by Allyson Smith and it's called the 7-Minute Life. In many ways, it's similar to my own Elevate Your 8 concept, and the two complement each other very well. What I like about this method that you do a huge brain dump of what positive actions you can take during that day to achieve your goals and then select the most important. And then I add the Pomodoro Technique to it all and BOO-YAH! I am one productive girl boss.

What's the Pomodoro Technique, you ask? It's not sauce for your pasta, although there is a tomato-like inspiration. The Pomodoro Technique is a time management method that uses a timer to break down work into intervals of focus and rest. These intervals are called "pomodoros" (or "tomatoes" in Italian), after the tomato-shaped kitchen timers that work perfectly for timing sessions. Pomodoros are separated by short breaks for distractions, daydreaming, snacking (or walking, which is what I do)... whatever.

It works like this:
- Choose a task to work on exclusively for twenty-five minutes.
- Set a timer for twenty-five minutes.
- Work on that task until the timer rings.
- Take a five-minute break.
- Repeat this cycle four times, and then take a

fifteen-minute break.

If I'm "chunking" my day making those appointments with myself (controlling my calendar, remember?), then I can take a two-hour chunk and break it into four work sessions. Some tasks I'll easily finish in the twenty-five minutes and some will require a second cycle. When I work this system I find that I am incredibly productive and I steam through my seven-minute ice actions for the day. I can usually just roll with one of these two-hour blocks in a day, but sometimes I'll do two—one in the morning and one in the afternoon if I am not busy with meetings.

There are dozens and dozens of apps, websites, and other articles dedicated to the Pomodoro Technique and timing (the above is from The Muse), and I have a favorite app. MinimaList is a complete rockstar app because it combines a to-do list with a built-in Pomodoro timer. You pull down to add a task and then click on the task to bring up your timer. Click "start" and it starts counting down. It will even tell you to put the phone down and get to work! After your session, it will time your break AND ask you if you completed the task. The app will also sync with your calendar so you can see where meetings fit into the day. I have been using this app for about a year now and it just adds to my ability to make sense of my day. I seldom look at my standard Outlook Calendar or Calendar app on my phone—MinimaList tracks it all for me; and I make sure that anything on my seven-minute life actions is reflected there.

There are two severely offensive productivity black holes out there and they both can be found on your computer: email and the Internet.

(Cue the suspicious crime movie music here.)

* * *

My email inbox had been the bane of my existence for YEARS. I've heard of inbox zero and the whole respond-file-delete thing but I could not get it to work until I used Pomodoro to monitor my email every day. I was at a place where I had anywhere between eighty to one hundred unread messages in my box and a total of close to four thousand messages in my box. It got so bad one year that I had to email IT and ask them to increase my storage because my inbox was constantly full (they did it for me but also told me to get my info under control—which still took about two more years, jeez).

As part of my "5 before 11" from the seven-minute life, I always write down EMAIL. At some point in the morning, I will get my Pomodoro timer ready, open my work email, and press "start." Then I go through every unread message that I can. I read it, respond, and file/delete. If there's no response needed it's straight to delete. I am NOT going to be that person who always says "Thank you" for responding to me or vice versa. If I don't get through all the unread messages, then I'll check my timer quickly for the last five minutes and make sure that the oldest emails get checked. Then I close the email and get to the next thing on my list. I will repeat this cycle ONE MORE TIME after lunch depending on the projects and meeting schedule for the day.

Twice a day for twenty-five minutes each. That's all you need to stay ahead of your email.

Unless you work in politics or a health and safety field, I'm pretty sure that no one is going to die or get fired if you do not respond to their email until the next morning or after lunch. And if it's that serious, they will call you or come to your office. Even during a global pandemic.

DRAWING THE LINE IN THE SAND

The reason most people tell me that they can't Elevate Their 8 is that they don't have enough time during a regular workday to get their job done. And I do not believe this one bit. If you are using the productivity and scheduling tools listed in the sections above, you'll already be on your way a bit. But there's a whole lot more going on here that you need to be aware of.

Part of finding balance in your day job has to do with how you approach to lunch, leaving the office, and communicating with your supervisor. These things are relatively easy once you set up some boundaries and draw a line in the sand that you do not cross. This takes time, patience, honesty, and holding your ground without being an asshole. It's doable, I promise you.

Lunch

Raise your hand if you've ever eaten at your desk

during your designated lunch hour in the hopes of getting more work done.

(Hand raised.)

And I used to beat myself up for this because I would dive into the total "multitasking" thing and prided myself on being able to do two or three things at once.

And we know for real… there's no such thing as multitasking. Our brains weren't meant to handle this much stimulus with any detail. So what we are doing is switch-tasking: going back and forth between the two tasks without very much focus or clarity on either.

Rudy Vidal from HuffPost said this about the brain and multitasking: "A 2013 study shows that high cognitive load severely impairs performance, especially when accurate and complex judgments are needed. Another study says that if you increase the number of things to which the brain needs to pay attention, it results in bottlenecks that can block awareness of important information and disrupt your ability to make decisions. In short, doing two or more tasks at once usually leads to impairment in at least one of them."

Trying to eat that gyro sammie while you finish your TPS reports is going to mean one of two things—that report won't be clear to you (or anyone else) at all, or you'll have tzatziki sauce all over your shirt or even the report!

If you handle your lunch break appropriately, you can not only fuel yourself and do something fun, but you can rock out some of your side hustle and maybe even take a quick walk. We'll cover this more in-depth in the next chapter; but here are the non-negotiable tenants of lunch:

* * *

- You must schedule it. Every day.

- You must TAKE it. Every day

- You must GET THE FUCK OUT of your office for lunch. Every day.*

- You must limit your lunches out with friends to once a week.

*In the Covid-19 world, this can be a little difficult, the whole "getting out" thing. So separate as best you can. We've covered schedule already, but now you've got to take that lunch. By taking lunch away from your office, you can already treat it as an appointment. Give yourself travel time, too. And while you're learning to balance the day job with the side hustle, you must bring your lunch to work. You can't waste the time of driving to a takeout place, driving back, and then forcing the food down before going back to work. Been there, done that. It gives me gas. You've got to find a place in your building that's a safe place for taking lunch. Is there a conference room you can schedule? An empty kiosk or cubicle? What about an official break room (my spot of choice) or a lunchroom? Whatever that space is, go there and remove yourself from your regular workspace. You need that time to relax and eat comfortably, but you'll possibly use the lunch hour for a few other things.

You can "chunk" your lunch up into fifteen, twenty, or thirty-minute segments (and I am assuming you have a full hour for lunch). Then assign tasks to those chunks. I have done all three of these with some variations over the years. I like to knit, watch TV, take a short walk, AND eat my amazing food during this downtime. Not so much the TV anymore; these days I'm taking online courses (like the one that helped me write this book) that are divided up into short manageable chunks—rather than TV shows, which are usually almost a full hour. And then, of course, I never want to stop, I want to keep going. Especially with

Billions and House of Cards.

I set timers for my various tasks—twenty minutes to enjoy my meal and maybe read something; twenty minutes of knitting (ask me about my shawl that I'm working on), and twenty minutes of an online course. Then I pack up my stuff and head back to my desk. I may pass on the knitting some days and take a walk outside.

I treat lunch as a highly sacred part of my workday because it's truly my time and I have learned how to make it a very productive time. You can as well now that you have these tips. It's quite amazing how productive an hour can be when you commit to it.

Scott Morris from SkillCrush.com published a lovely blog post in which he interviewed other 9 to 5 Side Hustlers and compiled their top tips. He refers to "UpSkill on Your Lunch Break" as a chance to learn new skills that will help you in the side hustle—and may even apply to your day job, too. He gave an example featuring Shannon Mattern, the CEO of a WordPress training site. In her years of running the marketing, continuing education, and IT departments for a small nonprofit, she was able to recognize the value of Wor Press in her self-taught pursuit of the software, which eventually led to a lucrative small business of her own.

Side note on WordPress—here's a great example of my own that turned the tables! It was teaching myself WordPress for both of my side hustles that led to a seamless transition for a content website that I manage in my day job. The designers were able to just share the link and the login details and I was off to the races. No training needed. You're very welcome, boss lady (insert smiley face here)!

Heading Home for the Day

Raise your hand if you've ever been right on the brink of going home when Pushy Paula stops by your desk to ask you something and will not shut up.

(Hand raised.)

There are so many things that can trip up to our ability to get out of the office when we want. Tricky colleagues can be one of those things. So can late afternoon meetings, a particularly troublesome project, or a phone call from your boss (you really can't manage the phone call from the boss, but I do provide hints on that later in this chapter).

In the section on scheduling, I talked about not putting meetings on your calendar that go past the end of your day—so don't do that. You could even set an appointment for yourself to process the day and set up for tomorrow. I do this! I have an appointment from four-fifteen to four-thirty p.m. that says, "prepare for tomorrow." I do these specific things before I end the day:

- Check my calendar for the next day.
- Put my planner on my keyboard.
- Put all the piles on my desk together so I have half-day clear, desk space.
- Turn off the computer.
- And then I grab my bag, hit the ladies' room and it's Kaiser Soze time—POOF—I'm gone.

Now and then, my supervisor will call me on the phone during the last half hour of the day—this is usually because she attends SO many meetings that this is free time where she can think. And I love my boss, but these late-day conversations can go on and on if I don't stay in control of them. So when the call comes, I do answer the phone.

Here's the dialogue:

Boss: "Oh good, you're still here."
Me: "I was just on my way out."
Boss: "Can you swing by here before you go?"
Me: "Is it something that can wait until tomorrow?"

If she says no, then I make sure to take all my stuff with me to her office, so the appearance of being ready to go home is real and felt. This isn't rude or manipulative—this is me owning my desire to finish my day and head home.

If she says yes, then I ask her what it's about so I can prepare accordingly. She'll tell me and I'll put a quick sticky note on my planner with the topic so I don't forget to connect with her.

A chatty colleague may try to bend your ear as you are on your way out of the office. This can usually look like this:

* * *

Colleague: "You got a minute?"
Me: "Actually I was on my way out."
Colleague: "It'll only take a minute."
Me: "Sure, but I'm going to use the ladies' room first."

Upon returning to the desk, I remind my colleague that I'm heading out, and is this something we can chat about tomorrow? And the sticky notes are sometimes used again.

You may be sitting and reading and thinking, "McPeak, you are not a very nice person." This isn't about nice. This is about managing my day so that I can work my eight hours and move on to the next part of the day. This isn't about being rude to my colleagues. This is about helping them manage their day as well. If I'm role modeling how I get out of the office at four-thirty p.m. each day, I'm showing them that it's doable. And it is, my friends. It is.

* * *

Talking to the Boss About Your Hustle

This is not meant to be a book about how to talk to your boss about difficult things. And I could write that book. Remember, I've had nine different jobs at nine different colleges in seven different states. And in some cases more than one boss at each job. I have officially decided this makes me an expert.

I am incredibly blessed in my current gig because I have at the BEST boss in the world. She looks out for her team, she is someone who trusts the staff to do their work, but she is not afraid to put it all on the table and kick the shit out of you with all love and admiration. I mean that. When you read the chapter on Lessons Learned, you'll understand.

Does this put me at an unfair advantage? Maybe. But it wasn't always this way. I'm not going to say that you must have the Greatest Boss in the World to be successful with your nine to five AND the side hustle. But I'm not going to lie—it does help.

I truly believe that having a strong, healthy relationship with your supervisor is the key to being happy at ANY job—unless you happen to have amazing colleagues or great staff. At my very last college housing position, I had a very tough time with my supervisor, but the folks for whom I was the supervisor were the best staff team I ever had. And being with them every day made up for having a tough boss. So there is some give and take—but at some point in the relationship, you'll probably need to have a difficult conversation. Navigating your side hustle with your day job may be one of those conversations, especially if they overlap in any way.

Let's say you work at a discount store. You're a shift manager. Your passion is music, so you play in a band on the weekends. It would certainly help for you to only work Monday through Friday, so you have the weekends to perform with your band (the side hustle). But remember, you work at a discount store—everyone probably wants weekends off. So you decide to schedule a meeting with your supervisor to discuss your request.

The best way to navigate these conversations is to know exactly what you are asking for, provide a rationale for it, and then indicate how you will continue to add value to the organization when you receive it. Notice my positive mental attitude by saying "when" rather than "if?" You can't go into this conversation automatically thinking that the boss will say no. If you do, they will most definitely say no. You want to exude confidence without being cocky. You want to be respectful without looking like a total brown-noser. And you don't want to go to that meeting ready to put out an ultimatum. This is a business conversation that you are going to navigate in the best interests of both parties.

* * *

One: What Do You Want?

Two: Why Do You Want It?

Three: What Is the Added Value or Compromise?

Four: How Do We Revisit the Agreement If It's Not Working?

Starting with the first question—what do you want? You want weekends off. Why? To rehearse and play with your band. Thus, you will propose to have three weekends off per month and that you will work both Saturday and Sunday on the fourth weekend. The added value is that you will work collaboratively with the other teammates who look for weekends off to switch shifts and help out when life events may occur, emergencies, etc. You offer to take on a special project that is usually done on the weekends and you come up with why it can be done during the week and your regular shift. And then finally—you agree with your boss to revisit the agreement after six weeks, obtain their feedback, and move forward. You also agree to ask your teammates now and then if they are finding the compromise to be helpful.

Standard negotiation and teamwork. You aren't just asking for a favor, you are submitting ideas on how your request can be accommodated and you are agreeing to compromise. And then you had better freaking keep all your agreements and don't take advantage. You got what you want, so don't screw it up.

The previous example is one of those "best-case scenarios" when everyone got what they wanted and should be better off because of it. But that may not be what happens during your first go around. Or, your supervisor may snub you from the get-go. And actually, you should have a fairly good gauge of how your supervisor will respond if you are an engaged employee. If you are NOT one of those, or if you are even possibly a troubled employee, then you might want to work on your day job before you go asking time off for your side hustle. Those who provide the most value to the organization are going to find themselves more likely to be in the good graces of the boss. So always make sure you are adding value and avoid making yourself expendable.

And then, what if you did everything right, including being a model employee in the first place, and your boss still says no? Then you need to find another place to have your balance. In our discount-store-weekend-band scenario... you didn't get three weekends off a month, you barely got one! Time to talk to the band and find out where the flexibility may lie. Can you rehearse on a weeknight now? Find clubs and shows that take place on weeknights as well? Or, can you find a coworker or Vital Work Friend (read Tom Rath's book "Vital Friends" to learn about this) who will switch shifts with you once a month? Be clever and creative, but don't break any rules or make your boss upset. See how things go, and then try again in six months.

My first live-off job in campus housing was in Chicago, Illinois, my hometown, and my favorite city in the world. When my husband landed a position as a bar manager, he convinced his boss to add a karaoke to their weeknight entertainment lineup, but they had to make ME the host. The manager agreed and my cousin's boyfriend came round with the equipment and POOF—I became a contract employee of a karaoke company. The bar would pay the karaoke company and he would pay me.

However, most urban bar and nightclub locations do not hold karaoke nights early. My show was Wednesday evenings from ten p.m. to two a.m. When I think about that now and my current lifestyle, I get just a bit nauseated (I wake up at four a.m. and go to sleep at eight p.m.). In those days, I was still in my thirties and was a complete and total karaoke junkie. That show was my entire social life. I love, love, loved it.

Housing can be a high-touch job and if you are not square with your supervisor and your teammates, then a scenario like this could be trouble. Especially if you enjoy an adult beverage or two with your karaoke friends. I was lucky that my colleagues were almost always willing to take my pager on Wednesday nights (yes, a pager. And later, a Nextel "click to talk." Don't judge). My supervisor was very understanding and did not schedule early meetings for Thursdays. He even allowed one of his going-away parties to happen at my show when he got a new job. And I am not going to make light of this—I was extremely lucky. As I look at my career now, almost twenty years later, I am amazed at the things that I had the balls to pursue in my late twenties and early thirties. I wonder what I would have done if one of my employees approached me with the same information. Would I have been as trusting and supportive? I might... then again, I might not.

Girlboss.com shares a great article on that balance between the side hustle and the day job, particularly if you do have a plan to make your side hustle your full-time job one day. That's not the main crux of this book, but I love what this post had to say, that I wanted to share it here.

Specifically, the article talks about being a model employee. Showing up physically and mentally for your full-time work every day. Giving that job and your coworkers your best effort and attitude. When you are at the day job, you gotta "be here now," and turn the volume down on that voice in your head that's saying, "a new podcast about..." and so forth. You need to keep on doing the work, stay humble, and focused. Keep your commitment to doing excellent work. Thanks, girl boss!

Digging Deeper...

- Which of the strategies discussed in this chapter seems the easiest to implement? Which will be harder for you?

- What usually is happening in your life for you to say to someone, "I don't have time"? Think about this one—because when you know exactly how you use that response, you'll be able to think more intentionally when you answer.

- How will you prioritize your tasks during the day so you can make the most out of your eight hours in the office?

Lessons Learned....

Even as I'm reading this over myself for the hundredth time and reviewing this particular section, I am scared to death to share this with you.

This "Lesson Learned" was one of the most difficult work problems I've ever had to face, admit, and resolve. It's one thing knowing that you made mistakes that need to be corrected—it's another to know that you've let your teammates down.

This day job of mine... I freaking love it. I love everything about it. The staff, the day-to-day tasks, the organization, the skill sets I learn and develop, and the rockstar relationship that I have with my supervisor. And it breaks my heart to think that I almost threw it away because of the attitude and practices I had assumed.

* * *

Which is absolutely why it belongs in this book.

The hardest thing about finding the balance between day job and side hustle, for me, was drawing the line. Drawing the line between when I'm at my day job and when I'm working my side hustle. And as I am writing that phrase I know how completely ridiculous it sounds. It's just obvious, right?

Well, yeah, it was. It IS. But I blew that off in the name of "management privilege."

When I became a salaried employee, that whole, "it doesn't matter when you get the work done, just get it done," mentality took over. And I hooked my behavior to that. In the beginning, it wasn't so much of an issue. As a hall director, you might have a late night, so you come in late the next day. Or if you work an entire weekend at an orientation travel program, and you take Monday and Tuesday off. You get the picture.

As a manager, I've worked under different supervisors who had different philosophies. There was a "mental health day." And the "once you work five hours, you've worked a full day." Or, "If you're going to take a half-day, just leave at one p.m. and don't take a vacation." And I share all this with you not to suggest that my previous supervisors were unethical. But they all had different interpretations of rules and regulations.

When I launched the swim team with my husband, I did print flyers for the team from my office. I used my work laptop to send emails, write memos, design Instagram posts with Canva. I didn't think much of this because I'd never been told anywhere that I couldn't check my email at work. And I'm also pretty sure I'm not the only person on the planet whoever did that.

* * *

My justification for all of it was that I wasn't making any money at the moment for the swim team, and I wasn't using my position to promote the swim team. I would just occasionally do some swim team business in the middle of the workday. During lunch, during a break, etc.

Looking back on all of it now, I cringe. Especially knowing what I know now about the appearances of things when I made my awful mistake. Oh boy, was it a dilly.

I started my blog before I started my podcast. No big deal. Just some writing here and there. No software to download. Write, copy, and paste posts. No big deal. I saved some stock images on my work computer, but I used those for work, too. I was multitasking, letting some aspects of day job interact with a side hustle (and this is something you'll hear me talk about again, in a more positive and uplifting way).

Then... along came the podcast and I fucked... up... royally.

My first few episodes were recorded at home. I had a laptop to use finally and I taught myself GarageBand and how to use Libsyn. I taught myself how to do A LOT of stuff. But finding the time at home to record when it was quiet became an issue. And I didn't want to ask or tell Charles that he should go outside or that I was closing a door while I was recording.

So... against my better judgment, I started recording at work. At the day job. I had ALL my podcasting equipment on hand, stored in a cabinet in my office until I needed it. In the beginning, I was just coming in early, recording outside of work hours. Putting everything away before the workday began. And that seemed to be going fine.

Honestly, I wasn't trying to hide anything from anybody. I was just trying to be super productive one day a week by doing someplace I knew would be quiet. My office, at six a.m., was very, VERY quiet.

But then I started booking interviews; and while people on the East Coast were totally happy to schedule for nine a.m. and ten a.m. their time, many West Coast people were not. So, I pivoted a little. I scheduled one or two interviews now and then during the workday. I would just close my door, conduct the interview, then put everything away. Except when I wouldn't. Sometimes I would move between listening to and editing the show while checking work email, writing/working on a project, or doing scholarship-based work. I was multitasking and I don't believe in multitasking. Because there is no such thing as multitasking. So both the show and my day job tasks were getting the shaft.

* * *

As I write this now, I want to throw my computer across the room because I feel such shame and guilt for what I was doing. It was so unlike me to give a mediocre effort across the board to things that I ENJOYED doing. Nonetheless, I was doing that.

But since no one was saying anything or complaining, I kept going. And I started conducting more interviews, going live on Facebook, and even creating mid-roll and pre-roll during work hours. I was still getting my work done, but it was not my best effort. Of course, I didn't fully realize this, I just kept turning things in and apologizing for missing deadlines. And, oh yeah, now and then giving my teammates a hard time when they would send something back to me because it was poorly executed or remind me of a deadline that I'd missed. And I was so entrenched in what I was doing, that I missed all of the signs.

ALL of them. No one was complaining. They weren't complaining to me… *they were complaining to my supervisor.*

Well, the day of reckoning arrived and I had one of those "Come to Jesus meetings" with my supervisor. And God love my boss, she is the most amazing woman in the world, she laid everything out to me in a way that was not only kind but firm, it was coming from a place of love because she saw that I was not myself. That I was crossing a line I had yet to draw because I was in completely unchartered territory and didn't think enough of what I was doing to pursue this ahead of time. Suffice to say, I cried a lot that day, but I also took copious notes because I did not want to let her down. I wanted to change—I NEEDED to change. Because if I fucked up again, I might just be gone. As a manager, I'm an at-will employee. I had no retreat rights. I serve at the pleasure of the president. And when she slid over the LITF ("letter in the file") that I was to read and sign, I thought it was over.

Thankfully, I received another chance. It was a very firm and specific chance—you must remove all your podcasting equipment and computer, you must not use non-work social media during the workday, you cannot come in early for anything other than day-job business, et cetera, et cetera.

I dodged a bullet but I learned an incredibly valuable lesson if I had only stopped to think about what I was doing. When you give two things half of your attention and attitude, you wind up giving nothing to both. Drawing that very clear line about when I'm doing the day job and when I'm doing the side hustle was paramount to improving my productivity and output on both sides of the coin.

Here are just a few tips I'd like to share in terms of

keeping it honest and straightforward in drawing and holding that line:

1. **Just. Don't. Do it.** Don't run any of your side hustle stuff from your day job. It's a bad, bad idea.

2. **Check your HR policies about all of this stuff.** Read every handbook. Peruse the website. Review any annual contract that you sign. In the days and weeks that followed this experience, my supervisor suggested that I could use the break room during lunch if I wanted to work on my personal computer.

3. **Be honest with your supervisor so they know you are pursuing a side hustle.** If you have a great relationship with your supervisor, he or she may applaud you and want to know more. My boss does fully support what I'm doing (especially now that my skill sets are running together in a few ways, more on that later).

* * *

(The main caveat with #3 is if you have a downright horrid relationship with your supervisor. If he/she is not supportive and/or you are on any sort of rocky ground at the day job, then you may be doing yourself a favor to stay silent. Find a mentor ASAP!)

4. Leverage your vacation days for your side hustle. I'll go into more detail in the next section. This has been a great way to not only focus on my side hustles and be productive with my podcast, but it's helped immensely with making sure I use all my vacation days. In 2018 I learned that I had stopped accruing for SIX MONTHS because I hadn't been taking time off. WTF! That was a lesson in fucking paying attention, but also became a key strategy for working my side hustles.

I have to say, while this experience was unpleasant, sad, and shameful, I wound up strengthening my relationship with my supervisor and I learned what I think is the key to balancing your day job with your side hustle…

… wait for it….

CLEAR AND CONCISE SEPARATION.

I felt so much better once I brought ALL my equipment and materials home and laid them out on my bed. But what in the Sam Hill was I going to do with all this STUFF? How was I going to manage now that I had to everything at home?

I needed a plan.

The answer came to me as my hubby was putting together a vanity space in our bedroom. He had found a couple of armoires at a yard sale—that match—and he stained and finished them. In between the furniture, he installed a flat tabletop, hung a mirror, and put up some track lighting. It is an adorable little space. HOWEVER, the track lighting began to fail right around the time that I brought all my equipment home. And thus, the vanity space became a podcasting and writing desk. I truly believe that the universe was putting out a sign on this, the timing was so crazy. Now, it's a tiny space and it can get cluttered when I am feeling slightly unorganized (which happens, I am not perfect); but my laptop, podcasting microphone, and mouse/mousepad fit perfectly there! Clear and concise separation, check!

So, yeah, lesson learned. A really big one. This experience was painful, frustrating, and heartbreaking... and it was one of the best things that have ever happened to me in finding that balance between day job and side hustle.

And Still Digging Deeper...

◆ What will "clear and concise separation" look like for you in this balancing quest?

- How will you leverage your vacation days as you move further into your side gig?
- Do you feel like you can be honest with your supervisor about your side hustle? Why or why not?
- Where might you find a mentor if you need one during this time?

Balance in the Side Hustle

This is where the rubber meets the road. You've got your day job in check and things are running smoothly. You're in at nine and out at five. You're crazy productive all day and you're happier at the day job than you ever were. So we're ready to go.

Even as I write this, I am very aware that I have made, and will continue to make mistakes and fall on my ass from time to time. And you pick the appropriate quotation for those moments. I like what Albert tells Bruce Wayne in BATMAN BEGINS:

"Why do we fall? So we can pick ourselves up again."

As I've worked my way to a routine and a process that has worked for me, I'm very aware that things change, we pivot, or we get inspired to do new things. You will experience this, too. And there will be days where you want to throw it all away and just go back to the day job and maybe a movie now and then.

I'm sure you've also heard the adage about this stuff is a marathon and not a sprint. It's a serious marathon… an ultramarathon. NO ONE starts a side hustle and is a millionaire within a few weeks —and if they are, then they are either really lucky or they did something questionable. Which is not my place to judge, that is just my opinion. I'm not a millionaire—yet.

Finding the balance in this side hustle takes a good amount of attention and restraint. It's like when I first learned to knit. I was AWFUL. I mean, really awful. Dropped stitches, uneven rows, you name it. But I kept at it because I was loving it. And you'll find this out as you progress in your side hustle, too.

* * *

In my case with knitting, it started to come before everything else. Before movies (although not always, I have knit in the movie theater before), before training for races, and before sex. I lived fiber and needles nonstop. I knit during STAFF MEETINGS sometimes.

The point here is that too much of a good thing can derail your productivity and health. I mean, I love ice cream but too much of that will give me a bellyache and other things. I love running, but too much of that will make me sore. We're looking for the right balance of the right activities for the right time.

"Easy for you to say, McPeak... you're already a few years in your business." This is true. But I had to find my routine and you will too. And even to this day, from time to time, I still find myself making Instagram posts on Canva past my bedtime… and you know what? I pay for that the next day because I'm not as sharp during my workout or my meditation time. Do you feel me?

So let's start easy, okay?

Your Side Hustle Activities

(If you want to use the official worksheets for this chapter, please visit www.krismcpeakcom/9to5book.)

Get out your notebook or some paper or a journal or open a Google Doc, OR you can use the official worksheets. Find a quiet place where you can focus on your side hustle. You aren't WORKING just now—you're preparing your balance strategy for your side hustle.

Write down ALL the activities that you perform when working on your side hustle. You can let this be all messy and brainstorm-y if you want, or you can create a refined list. Here is mine:

1. Website Development

2. Creating Social Media

3. Scheduling and posting Social Media

4. Engaging on Social Media

5. Product Development and Creation

6. Scheduling Podcasts

7. Recording Podcasts

8. Editing and posting podcast episodes

9. Marketing podcast episodes

10. Working with clients

11. Communicating with my audience (email)

12. Finances

13. Blogging

14. Writing this book

15. Professional Development (courses, coaching, mastermind group)

This is only what I do in my side hustle, SilverPeak Development. I'm going to leave out what I do for the swim team, SilverPeak Performance, as I don't want to overwhelm you. You're welcome.

Now I'm going to go back to this list to rank them in order of most enjoyable to least enjoyable. Here we go:

Most Enjoyable

1. Product Development and Creation
2. Recording Podcasts
3. Editing Podcasts
4. Writing this Book
5. Professional Development
6. Working with Clients
7. Creating Social Media
8. Engaging on Social Media
9. Blogging
10. Scheduling and Posting Social Media
11. Marketing podcast episodes
12. Website Development

13. Communicating with my audience (email)

14. Finances

15. Scheduling Podcasts

Least Enjoyable

If we break this down just a bit, I think it's obvious that I love the creative process and don't so much like the administrative or production work. And what I learned during my second post-master's professional position was that the things I loved got all my energy and the things I didn't love waited until the end. And were usually not completed on time or very well (well, would YOU like judicial meetings more than events and programming? I thought not).

The point is that you should determine times in your week to work on your side hustle when you have certain energy flow. So for me, that means finances, email, and web development need to be done when I'm not likely to be disturbed and when I have good energy. So that's either in the morning before I launch my regular morning routine, or in the evening before dinner but after walking the dog. So I schedule those things accordingly.

*. *. *. *. *

Research and Practice

I'm taking a quick sidebar here to share with you how I determined when I should do some of these low-energy, not-fun-for-me activities. Because once I knew this stuff, I felt so much more productive in my side hustle, it was amazing.

There is a really neat online product and blog called CoSchedule. They are a paid service but have a great deal of free content and tools. One of my very favorites is the Best Time to Send Email Based On 14 Studies blog post and online tool. You can request their "Best Time to Send Email Kit" and do this research for yourself. Which I have done… twice.

* * *

CoSchedule's initial information states that the best DAYS to send emails are Tuesdays, Thursdays, and Wednesdays, in that order. From there they break down the best times: six a.m., ten a.m., two p.m., eight p.m.. The kit mentioned above gives you a worksheet to use so you can track your emails. It's incredibly easy to use and quite fun. What I learned in both situations is that six a.m. on Tuesday is when my emails get the most opens and clicks. So that's what I shoot for.

Since preparing emails and scheduling them is one of my least favorite things to do, it needs prime time in my day. Monday mornings first thing doesn't work for me because it's the beginning of the new week; so it's Monday evenings post-dog-walk-pre-dinner. About five-thirty p.m., My iPhone has a recurring alarm that goes off at five-thirty p.m. on Mondays. BANG. I crank out that email, schedule it, and enjoy the amazing dinner that has been prepared by my hubby.

* * *

Finances. Fuck. I hate money. Years and years of fiscal fiascos. But it has to be done. And since I run a swim team with my hubby where there is a hell of a lot more money conversations and work to have, that work is scheduled for Wednesdays, post-dog-pre-dinner. And since Coach Husband doesn't have workouts on Wednesday evenings, we do finances together for the swim team. Then if I have my stuff to do, I work it in. Again, a recurring alarm on my phone for Wednesdays at five-thirty p.m.

Now it's time to hammer out the other stuff. I am part of a wonderful female coaching group called SOCA (Stand Out Coaching Academy) led by Lindsay Maloney. During the academy part of my studies, there was a section called "Like a CEO." This was an activity where you chose your workdays and times and inserted what work was going to get done. My journey was inspired by this exercise—I just started by getting the crappy stuff out of the way first.

On the book page on my site (www.krismcpeak.com/9to5book), you can download a similar type of activity. The gist is this....

How many hours a week do you want to work on your side hustle? In the beginning, there may be many hours, because you are excited and want to dig in as much as possible. I would advise against this... it's not a sprint, right? It's a marathon. And you don't sprint out of the starting gate for a marathon. You get your warmup miles in first.

Earlier in the book, when we talked about the Elevate Your 8 Philosophy, you might have completed the Time Block Exercise online that helped you see where all your time was going. And part of the Elevate Your 8 Philosophy includes making time for everything and prioritizing. So starting a side hustle is not about just working your day job, your biz, and nothing else. It's about balancing it all. That's why you're reading this book!

I would recommend four to six hours a week to start. Roughly one hour a day during the workweek or a few extra hours on the weekends. You've got to continue making time for your other hobbies, interests, and relationships or you'll lose them. And while I believe in the concept of a "vocation," or "calling," when it comes to meaningful work; but you are more than that as a human being. Are we clear?

Now, back to the worksheet. Choose your initial work hours for your side hustle. The total number of hours and when. Here is what mine looked like to start:

* * *

Monday: 1 hour (5:30 p.m. - 6:30 p.m.)

Tuesday: 1 hour (4:30 a.m. - 5:30 a.m.)

Wednesday: 1 hour (5:30 p.m. - 6:30 p.m.)

Thursday: 1 hour (5:30 a.m. - 6:30 a.m.)

Friday: OFF

Saturday: 2 hours (12:00 p.m. – 2:00 p.m.)

Sunday: 2 hours (9:00 a.m. – 11:00 a.m.)

Now it was time to assign the various tasks to these business hours. What was I going to work on during each selected time? And you already know the answer to this. My more creative time is in the morning, so that's for product development, writing, and podcasting. Afternoons are for more administrative things:

Monday: Email Communication

Tuesday: Podcast Recording or Editing

Wednesday: Finances

Thursday: Other Content Creation (Blog Posts, Books, Courses)

Saturday: Catching up on tasks from the week*
Sunday: Social Media

*What's this? Following the Elevate Your 8 Philosophy, there should be some time allocated on the weekends to catch up from the previous week, fitting in "must-do" activities that were tabled or otherwise rescheduled to fit your priorities for the workweek. And I do this in the early afternoon because Saturday mornings are normally filled either with swim practice and social time or an open-water swim. And writing, like what I'm doing right now, takes place during other times that I carved after I'd been running my businesses for a while.

And these times were NOT originally set in stone. I had to do a great deal of trial and error to make them stick. I spend additional time now on my business as it's more incorporated into my morning routine. These days, I make time for writing, or you would not be reading this little content gem right now.

Flexibility is the key to balance (you'll learn more about that in the Semper Gumby chapter). And you will not perfect this routine immediately. It may take weeks, or months to make this stick.
But above all else, you MUST be consistent.

Leveraging Vacation Days

THIS has become the big secret to my success! And it happened by accident.

I'm pretty good at taking my vacation days anyway, but I still have a few here and there that rollover. So when I was first invited to be on the PodQuest Podcast with Michael Neely, I sent to his website and it seemed as though the only slots available were during the workday. Dang. I chose an eleven a.m. slot thinking that I'll just go to lunch early.

* * *

Then later that week I received the BIG email from my favorite author, Sarah Knight. I'd been trying to schedule her for my show for several weeks. Dealing with time zones and internet issues, and going back and forth via IGDM (that's Instagram Direct Message) and email… finally, she gave me a time that would work for her absolutely, no doubt.

Uh-huh. During the workday—SAME DAY as my interview with Michael Neely. Now I would have to take a vacation day because there was no way in hell that I was planning to try and reschedule Sarah Knight. Not my favorite author. No fucking way.

And thus, this practice was born. It worked like a DREAM. I can get four to five interviews done in a day and then they are pretty much batched for the month. I can then edit and prep show notes during the other slots of the week when I work on podcast business. I'm a fucking genius.

Well, at least I thought I was. It's a pretty simple idea but it would have never occurred to me to do this because vacation is—well, it's a vacation. And we don't work when we go on vacation. But in some cases, we do work on our side hustles. And this has become a practice that I can live with—and I do enjoy as well.

Kids

I was not originally planning to write a section on kids, because, you know, **I don't have any.** But a colleague of mine at the day job asked so I decided to investigate this a little. Like my daddy always said, "If you don't ask, you don't get." So I conducted a highly scientific study and posted on Facebook. I asked my buddies with children to expand a bit on how they manage to have their kids at home while they are working from home. Shit, I don't think I realized just how interesting all this COVID reflecting time could be. Gotta find those silver linings wherever we can, right?

In reviewing all these posts, I see how meaningful the pandemic has been in helping so many people juggle many balls and wear many hats—which is EXACTLY what a 9-to-5 Side Hustler must reckon with. Which makes it applicable to this book. Especially since, as you all know, I don't have kids.

These tips, suggestions, and experiences are coming DIRECTLY from my friends on Facebook, so they get full credit for all this stuff. THANK YOU all for contributing!

Chris Young—Residence Life Professional in Oregon

♦ Providing your kid with a semi-consistent schedule of things they need to do that day. It helps provide some structure. My list usually includes some chores and some reading/homework. It's pretty minimal, but it keeps her on track, and, admittedly, out of my hair so I can work uninterrupted for about an hour or two.

◆ Taking pause breaks to play and cuddle with the kiddo. This is partly because I have a great and understanding supervisor, but with social distancing and being home more, I've noticed my daughter wants more of my attention and love than before. So every hour or two I'll take a five- or ten-minute break to snuggle or play with her and that seems to help. Sometimes this turns into an hour break to go for a walk, but sometimes those breaks are needed (if they can be had).

◆ Leaving the nine-to-five mentality behind. There's no real way to balance parenting and working from home at the same time. So I just accepted that some of my work will have to be done differently. Now I wake up at four a.m. to get three to four hours of work done before she wakes up and gets the rest of my work time in throughout the day as much an I'm able.

◆ Rely on your community/quaran-team. When COVID-19 first took hold, I had a small, select group of neighbors/friends with whom we decided to quarantine together as a team. This helped give me some periodic reprieve and gave my daughter a social circle she could still safety play with periodically.

Douglas Ferguson—Advancement Professional in Pennsylvania

Schedule, schedule!

Emily Jenkins—Educator in Northern California

◆ My kids are three months, three years, and six, so we are juggling infant, preschool, and almost first-grader over here with Mom and Dad both working from home.

◆ We use Facetime to help give my husband and me a break. My mother-in-law has a weekly tea party with our six-year-old and her cousin. This is an hour she gets to spend hearing Grandma read a story, doing an art project together, and eating a fun snack. My mom also does one hour with each of my older two kids. She has ordered activity books and she has a copy at her house and sent a copy to our house so they can do fun activities together and both be looking at the same thing.

◆ Making an effort to keep a morning routine —if I don't I start to wonder when was the last time they brushed their teeth or took a shower 🙈 So I try to make sure everyone has a good breakfast and is dressed for the day, and then usually we take a walk around the neighborhood before I start in on work.

◆ We try to make sure that my husband or I take a break every hour or so and do something with the kids for ten to fifteen minutes. Sometimes that is making lunch together, which needs to be done anyway or playing a quick game.

◆ We set up a desk next to each of our workstations so that if I am on a call or doing work my three-year-old, for example, could sit at the desk next to me and color or build blocks. It makes him feel like he is right there and part of the action.

◆ Involving the kids in cooking as much as possible. I was finding that if I wrapped up work and started cooking dinner, they would go a little bonkers needing attention, but if I have them cook dinner with me it might create twice the mess and take twice as long, but they had a great time and it's good family bonding.

- Thankfully, I have the flexibility with work to adjust the hours I am working if one of the kids is having a hard day. I don't love having to put in hours at night when the kids are asleep because I need my wind-down time too, but sometimes it's necessary.

- Work outside. Luckily, my Wi-Fi reaches to our backyard, we have a large yard, and we have been able to set up a nice space for us to work while the kids play. For my kids, being outside is their happy place.

- We both also always try to be honest with any client calls we might have and start by saying that we are sheltering in place with our three children under six. Everyone is incredibly understanding and this helps remove the stress of worrying that they might hear a child in the background or not understand if you get briefly interrupted. I find being honest with people at the beginning of the call is much easier than having to explain if a three-year-old is suddenly crying.

◆ Introduce new things. I've tried to have a new puzzle or game or book every week or so just to help mix things up. Lots of library rentals and our library does bags every week with all the materials for a science activity.

◆ Laugh—if I don't laugh I'd cry, so I've tried to just let things go, be flexible, be patient, and forgiving with myself when we have a bad day and remember that this is just tough for everyone.

Digging Even Deeper...

◆ Try to start the process of becoming your CEO and work the exercise that I described earlier in this section. Which tasks are your favorite and which are your least favorite?

◆ How does it feel going through these exercises and putting a schedule together?

◆ For those of you with kids - how will you

come to balance that aspect of your life with work and side hustles?

Semper Gumby: Always Flexible
(As shared by Dr. Erika Endrijonas, during the Covid-19 Pandemic)

Veteran animator Art Clokey created Gumby, the lovable green creature made of clay, for his 1953 short film Gumbasia. Television executives loved the character so much, they granted him his own program, The Gumby Show. His unusual shape and claymation movements made him a unique character. Clokey later admitted that the unusual shape of Gumby's head was modeled after one of the few surviving photos of his father, which shows him with a large wave of hair protruding from the right side of his head. In 1955, Gumby toys hit the market. The bendy action figure has become a prized classic in the toy world and has been a regular at toy stores since its introduction.

On March 9, 2020, I came to work with the mindset of many Americans. The coronavirus was spreading, but California wasn't being hit hard yet, and… yes, I was cracking a few jokes here and there, no big deal. It was not at all on my radar yet. But that would change quickly.

By Wednesday, March 11, I was talking to my colleague in the office (while our boss was on vacation, mind you) and commiserating on how the world seemed to be changing right before our eyes. The Spring Semester Flex Day was changed so that faculty could take a look at possible online courses if the college would close. Later that afternoon, my colleague and I called our boss, who was on vacation in Costa Rica with her family and let her know what was going down. On Thursday, March 12, my management colleague and I taught our team how to use Zoom.

On Monday, March 16, I sat in the gymnasium of my community college to observe social distancing while our superintendent/president shared options and thoughts about how we would move forward. And on that day, the term "Semper Gumby" was coined.

Always be flexible.

Everything that we knew about education, teaching, learning, etc., has been challenged because of the recent pandemic. I am beyond proud that I work for an institution of higher education that embraced Semper Gumby and moved to the next level of student services and student success. It was a rocky road but we are moving forward.

Which is pretty much the biggest lesson to be learned about balance between your day job and your side hustle. Things happen day to day that challenges us and makes us wonder, "how am I going to get past this?" Even as I'm writing this, I am facing challenges not only with the pandemic in my day job but in both my side hustles.

You've probably heard that word "pivot," right?

To pivot is to turn or rotate, like a hinge. Or a basketball player pivoting back and forth on one foot to protect the ball. When you're not talking about a type of swiveling movement, you can use pivot to mean one central thing that something depends on.

In the entrepreneurial world, a pivot is a buzzword referring to a significant business change ranging from mild to dramatic. In January of 2020, I set goals for the year with my business coach and mastermind teacher, Allison Melody. By mid-March of 2020, I was to be signed between eight to twelve career changes to a mastermind group and work toward earning myself about twenty thousand dollars. That was the plan I was shooting for. BANG. Pandemic took that out to a certain extent.

And so... pivot. Now I'm writing my third book and I'm loving every minute of it. Semper Gumby, dammit! (Channeling my inner Eddie Murphy there)

Some of the most profitable and successful businesses today started out as something different and made a pivot. They include, but are not limited to, YouTube, Groupon, Pinterest, Slack, and Instagram. In fact, YouTube was originally set up to be a DATING SITE. "Tune in, Hook up," was the slogan. Wow. According to Entreprenuer.com, "You don't have to be a hit right out of the gate to become a successful entrepreneur, nor does your business idea need to remain intact to maximize those chances of success. Instead, open your mind to other possibilities, and don't be afraid to make a major change -- even if you're already a few years in. It might just be the change you need to save the business."

As I write this book, I embrace Semper Gumby every day. I wake up, approach my morning routine, and move forward into my day. I knew I would write more books, but hadn't planned on that for this year. Jeez. And now, this book is becoming a rebranding plan for my business. And guess what? If that doesn't work, I'll pivot again. Because part of being an entrepreneur means that you must embrace the unknown; or as the great rock philosophers, REO Speedwagon, has said, "Roll With the Changes."

I know my fair share of people who get into side hustles because they want to latch on to a quick get-rich scheme and skip on into the sunset. I don't think anyone STAYS an entrepreneur if they think they were getting in on a get-rich-quick scheme. It's hard work, it's making sacrifices, and it's falling over and over and over again (just to pick ourselves back up). It is also rewarding, exciting, and allows you to learn something every day. And make a little money, too.

Keep On Digging:

- ◆ What tactics can you deploy in your day job and your side hustle to be more flexible?

- ◆ Have you already had to pivot? What was that like for you?

- ◆ Please email me at info@krismcpeak.com and tell me your pivot story!

You're a 9-to-5 Side Hustler!

This is a book for people who LOVE their 9 to 5 but WANT to pursue a little something extra that will serve as both extra income and something fun, enjoyable, and giving you a sense of service. You should be at this point now where you can look at your day job and your side hustle and say...."Okay, I'm feeling pretty good."

And the reason I wrote this book stems back to what Angie Gardner has to say about The Side Hustle in her book, TIME MILLIONAIRE:

A side hustle is a way to earn extra "Plan B" income that allows flexibility to pay off debt and/or enrich your lifestyle. It can also be your opportunity to delve into whatever you are most passionate about without quitting your full time job.

This is really what it's all about for me. I had

always wanted to make a little extra money to both make ends meet and maybe give myself a new pair of shoes (or a new swimsuit) every now and then.

But it couldn't be a grind. It couldn't be something I felt like I HAD to do. Such as selling cosmetics and hosting beauty parties. Some adults are all over that stuff. But I tried it and found it to be like beer - an acquired taste. I couldn't make that a permanent side hustle because I didn't love it. I didn't believe in it. Didn't want to sell it. Couldn't stand behind it.

The things I'm doing now in my business - with my podcast, writing books, and doing career coaching and online masterminds - this feeds my soul and is the perfect compliment to what I do in my day job. I've been working with students for over 25 years; and this little side hustle of mine is a way to keep doing that…and not just college students, but every type of student in every walk of life. We are all students of SOMETHING: sports, television, science fiction, self-help…time management, adulting, swimming…you get the picture.

I'm grateful to have had many of my friends and colleagues share some of their success tips with me for inclusion in this book. So, the conclusion will end with my contributors and I hope you glean just as much from their wisdom as you have from the whole book. Thank you for being part of this experience - and I look forward to hearing more about your side hustles and day job value.

Tamar Medford - Vancouver, BC - Outside Sales
(and host of "The Road to Health" Podcast)
My biggest success strategy for running a small business and holding down a regular 9 - 5 career has been planning and organization. I wasn't

always a morning person but realized after doing this for a while if I woke up a couple of hours earlier than I usually did, I could get most of my work done before starting my day. Starting first thing allowed me to become a lot more flexible at the end of the day in case anything went sideways. Working a job where I'm travelling a lot, you often don't know when your day is going to end, so planning my most essential activities, first thing in the morning meant nothing got put off until the following day and kept me on track.

One of the struggles I'm currently working to overcome is juggling my education and my work. I've done most of the work in getting my business up and running, so I've had to learn many things on my own and some of them by learning the hard way. This struggle has made planning even more critical. Although It would be great to be able to outsource many things I struggle to develop or create, there is a sense of joy that comes from taking the time to figure it out.

The longer I do this, the easier it has become, and I'm grateful for all the challenges that come along because I feel accomplished at the end of the day when I can figure things out on my own or with the help of others. Doing something I'm genuinely passionate about for my side hustle has changed my life in more ways than I could have ever imagined. It's given me an even greater reason for getting out of bed in the morning.

Janice McQueen-Ward - Santa Monica, CA - Training Manager
Pageant Coach and Host of Beauty Call Podcast

What have been your biggest success strategies and tips for running a small biz and working a 9 to 5?

I have a Pageant Coaching business, I host a podcast and do acting on the side. It is a lot to manage that and my 9 to 6 job, but I use Calendly to schedule my guests and my clients so that I have a set time in which to work. I also schedule in time for exercise and time for my husband. I find that the more I take care of myself and my family, the better I can balance the many side hustles. Prioritization and scheduling is the key to success. If I don't schedule it can make me feel out of control. When I set time aside to work on my dreams and goals, I no longer judge myself for not having time, as I am making time. What I am learning, especially this year, is to also say NO to some things, so that I can say YES to the right things.

What's been one big struggle that you haven't overcome yet?

My imposter syndrome. I tend to sometimes self-sabotage myself by either taking on too much or halting myself when I am very close to success. I am able to help others through their struggles, but battle this struggle myself.

Heidi Sheaks - Woodland Hills, CA - Owner of West Coast Cuts and Color (And Younique Sales Representative)

What have been your biggest success strategies and tips

for running a small biz and working a 9 to 5?

First of all is setting up priorities. My 9-5 job is nothing but beyond 9-5. My main so-called 9-5 job is my priority. I say "so called" since I work way past 5 pm and start thinking of tasks to do before 9 am. I have owned a hair salon for three years now and have worked there over 14 years. When starting to take over the salon I wanted and needed an emergency fund or savings. This is where my "side hustle" small biz came into play. I used to do makeup in the film industries and was wondering how I could bring in extra money to help offset financial fear as well as financial burden in taking on my " 9-5" Priority job. Someone approached me about make up sales and I thought this would align well . Younique was introduced to me first of all. I wanted to support a small business and I was in need of makeup. I tried the line and the offer was always presented to make this my side hustle. I tried out most of the products first before I even tried to think about selling it. It's a lot to do, owning basically two businesses without one overshadowing the other.

Tasks and check lists goals are key for both. I have a morning routine (like the author, I am a swimmer). And even though the coronavirus has gotten in the way, routine is key! When i decided to do my side hustle as well as run my salon beyond just the 9-5 i had to be persistent and consistent. So I would get to my main job at least an hour before opening so I can set things up. Not only for the salon, but if I had time to engage in a live video showcasing mascara, makeup, or skin care that would add to my engagement with customers.

I need to budget my time properly so that my main job would not suffer and I would not create an atmosphere to my co-workers that this side gig was priority over my main job, the salon. I did not want to create a unworthy work atmosphere in that the side gig was more important. I did not want my team to feel that they were required to buy things or promote my side hustle. The live videos gave me a way to engage with an audience and potential customers, but once it was time for the salon I transitioned.

One thing I love about my side gig is it's something I can always come back to if life happens and I put it on the back burner. It's always there, in the same way that I kept up on my hair licence while i was doing makeup for film and television. It was like insurance for a career, and something to always fall back on. No matter what side hustle you pursue, passion is a must. When people see your passion and what you believe in, you will be able to engage with them. When it comes to hair and makeup, my clients know that I know my stuff and can answer any questions they have.

What's been one big struggle that you haven't overcome

yet?

ORGANIZATION. Things like "list-making" are all good in thought, but I often get distracted and there you go. If I stop my routine and slack off even for one day, that will turn into two days. Then there is too much to do to try and catch up and be on point on both sides. I seem to slack off on the important personal touches that both businesses so badly need. Even though I make folders and print outs of tasks to do daily, after 11 hours at the day job, I would get tired. The side hustle takes a back seat. When I get behind, my anxiety and occasional imposter syndrome overcomes me and then I just focus on the main job. There is something to be said about accountability not only to team members but as well as to yourself. I do love having goals, projects and feeling accomplished.

Shelley Wasicki - Columbus, Ohio - Banking (owner of The Positive Spirit Co and co-owner of Franke's Photography)

I think my biggest success for navigating a

growing side hustle(s) was organizing my time. I have a full time job which is 40 plus hours, a company called The Positive Spirit Co. and a photography business, Franke Photography.

My biggest impact tool was putting items in time slots.

- Monday is my catch up night for my side hustles.
- Tuesday is my social media update night. While I try to post things sporadically, I have this time set aside specifically for managing my social media sites and upcoming web site.
- Wednesday And Thursdays's are slotted for The Positive Spirit Co. projects. I track my orders, progress of them, get shipping items together and physically make the products.
- Friday is my shipping day for TPSC and used to tie up any loose ends from the week. We sell our merchandise at a local artisanal shop , so this day and weekend a

are great for swapping out items that we have available.

If we've done a photo shoot, I like to pick away at my editing. I use the weekends for this or any free time during the week.

Prior to using this system, I felt overwhelmed and all over the freaking place with managing all three business aspects of my life. For me, this system was a game changer! (Side bar, I'm flexible with my calendar above, so if anything needs to be tweaked I have the ability to do so).

What I wish I had known before starting my side hustle?

I guess just finding a system that worked for me. Everyone's needs will be different depending on what their side hustle is. I had no idea how long it would take me to finish my projects, so once I nailed that down, things moved along more smoothly.

* * *

I'm excited to say that I am growing The Positive Spirit Co. so my hope is that it turns into my full time job within the year!!

Resources

There are links throughout the book where you can learn more from the references I quoted, but here's a list of books and websites I highly recommend, not just because they helped me write this book (and my other two!), but they are just GREAT resources!

I am an Amazon Affiliate, so any purchases you make as a result of these links may throw some loose change my way. Thanks!

Choose Yourself - James Altucher
Time Millionaire - Angie Garner
The $100 Startup - Chris Guillebeau
100 Side Hustles - Chris Guillebeau
Get Your Shit Together - Sarah Knight
You Do You - Sarah Knight
The Side Hustle - Nick Loper
You Are a Badass - Jen Sincero
Sleep Smarter - Shawn Stevenson
168 Hours - Laura Vanderkam

About the Author...

Kris McPeak is an author, educator, and podcaster and has worked in Higher Education for more than 25 years. A "Recovering Housing Professional," Kris started her career in College Housing and Residence Life before transitioning to Community College Advancement.

The Self-Appointed "Mary Poppins of Higher Education, " Kris has worked at 9 different colleges/ universities in 7 states over her 25 year career. Her husband is a very good sport.

"The 9-to-5 Side Hustler" is Kris' third book. She's also written, "Making 'Work' Work for You," and "Elevate Your 8." She hosts a weekly podcast, also called "Elevate Your 8." Kris' articles have been featured on Lifehack and CASE Currents and she's been featured on top-ranked podcasts since 2018.

When she's not writing, podcasting, or running her day job, Kris runs a non-profit US Masters Swim Team with her hubby, Charles McPeak. You can learn more about their team, SilverPeak Performance, at www.silverpeakperformance.com. She herself is a competitive swimmer with a long term goal of becoming a National Champion in the 200 yard Breaststroke.

Kris and Charles live in Southern California with their furry baby, Duke. She strives to be a vegan (ice cream is a problem), loves to knit and binge-watch TV, and is a mad karaoke junkie. Learn more at www.krismcpeak.com.